ROY THOMSON HALL

ROY THOMSON HALL
A PORTRAIT

WILLIAM LITTLER | JOHN TERAUDS

DUNDURN
TORONTO

Project Editor: Allison Hirst
Copy Editor: Jenny Govier
Design: Jennifer Scott
Printer: Friesens

Unless otherwise credited, photos are courtesy of Roy Thomson Hall.

Library and Archives Canada Cataloguing in Publication

Littler, William
    Roy Thomson Hall : a portrait / William Littler and John Terauds.

Includes index.
Issued also in electronic formats.
ISBN 978-1-4597-1875-3

1. Roy Thomson Hall--History. 2. Music--Ontario--Toronto--History and criticism. I. Terauds, John, 1963- II. Title.

ML205.8.T6L58 2013   780.9713'541   C2013-900775-X

1   2   3   4   5   17   16   15   14   13

We acknowledge the support of the **Canada Council for the Arts** and the **Ontario Arts Council** for our publishing program. We also acknowledge the financial support of the **Government of Canada** through the **Canada Book Fund** and **Livres Canada Books**, and the **Government of Ontario** through the **Ontario Book Publishing Tax Credit** and the **Ontario Media Development Corporation**.

Care has been taken to trace the ownership of copyright material used in this book. The author and the publisher welcome any information enabling them to rectify any references or credits in subsequent editions.

J. Kirk Howard, President

Printed and bound in Canada.

Visit us at
Dundurn.com
Definingcanada.ca
@dundurnpress
Facebook.com/dundurnpress

Dundurn	Gazelle Book Services Limited	Dundurn
3 Church Street, Suite 500	White Cross Mills	2250 Military Road
Toronto, Ontario, Canada	High Town, Lancaster, England	Tonawanda, NY
M5E 1M2	LA1 4XS	U.S.A. 14150

The Corporation of Massey Hall and Roy Thomson Hall gratefully acknowledges the support of The Woodbridge Company Ltd. and Jack McLellan, president of the Edwards Charitable Foundation, for underwriting the cost of this commemorative book and for their long and generous support of our halls.

The Toronto Symphony Orchestra has been known by various names. For its first five seasons it was known as the New Symphony Orchestra; starting in 1927–28 it was known as the Toronto Symphony Orchestra; in 1966 the name was changed to the Toronto Symphony; and in 1993 the name was changed back to the Toronto Symphony Orchestra. In this book, for the convenience of readers, the name Toronto Symphony Orchestra is used throughout.

CONTENTS

ACKNOWLEDGEMENTS

A S WITH ANY BOOK, especially one with a historical reach, *Roy Thomson Hall: A Portrait* has been a collective effort. Thanks are due to the many people who participated in the research, the writing, and the securing of graphic material.

The central team at the Corporation of Massey Hall and Roy Thomson Hall was led by Heather Clark, who encouraged the participation of many disparate hands, sometimes with bribes of chocolate or whatever else seemed to work. Peter O'Brien assisted with the final editing, negotiations with the publisher, and collecting the graphic material. Alexandra Basen ferretted out research and material of various sorts, sometimes well hidden in archival boxes. Janet Connolly started the research in the summer of 2011, and Keri Ferencz assisted with research, writing, and essential organizing of central source material.

Other staff who read earlier drafts, fed information to the writers and editors, or assisted in other ways include Elizabeth Birss, Cathie Carlino, Victoria-Lynn Cartwright, Charles Cutts, Derek Fast, Zita Griskonis, Laraine Herzog, Robin Howarth, Susan Jegins, Richard Kalitsis, Dan Kershaw, Jesse Kumagai, Mary Landreth, Basil Lowe, Carol Anne Lynch, Meghan McCready, Stephen McGrath, Stefania Paterak, Sarah Pomper, Karry Prendergast, Jamie Rodriguez, Colleen Smith, Lillian Thalheimer, Allan Webster, and Liew Wong.

Toronto Symphony Orchestra staff and volunteers who enthusiastically aided in the presentation of both the words and images include John Dunn, Loie Fallis, Laura Quinn, and Andrew Shaw. Paul Gardiner, of the City of Toronto Archives, unearthed various important images.

Gabriel Kney and Kevin Komisaruk were essential to capturing the story of the Roy Thomson Hall organ.

Suzanne Bradshaw, Jag Gundu, Nobuo Kubota, Keith Loffler, Alexander Mair, Andrea Mateka, Janice Price, and Nancy Westaway helped focus particular elements of this story.

A special thanks goes to all those who were interviewed for the book — their rich memories helped populate the coming pages with historical observations, personal anecdotes and stories, and clarification of dates, roles, and responsibilities. They include Patsy Anderson, Jean Ashworth Bartle, Larry Beckwith, Barbara Bellamy, Suzanne Bradshaw, Wende Cartwright, John Clappison, Heather Clark, Robert Cranston, Neil Crory, Charles Cutts, Andrew Davis, Terri Dunn, Eric Friesen, Douglas Gardner, Attila Glatz, Marion Glatz, Catherine Gregor, Loie Fallis, Piers Handling, Cynthia Hawkins, Walter Homburger, Susan Jegins, Kimber Jonah, Ross and Ann Kennedy, Jesse Kumagai, John Lawson, Keith Loffler, Tom MacMillan, Bill Neish, Jane Rowland, Pat Taylor, Lillian Thalheimer, Liz Tory, and Nancy Westaway.

John Lawson in particular deserves thanks for his patience with endless questions on early corporate history, and his ongoing interest throughout the various drafts of this book.

And thanks to copy editor Jenny Govier and the team at Dundurn: Beth Bruder, Margaret Bryant, Sheila Douglas, Jennifer Gallinger, Allison Hirst, Kirk Howard, Karen McMullin, Shannon Whibbs, and Britanie Wilson.

INTRODUCTION

"It Sounds Delightfully":
Toronto Grows Up with Music

I N THE EIGHTEENTH and early nineteenth centuries, Toronto, Montreal, Quebec City, and Halifax were garrison towns, dependent for much of their musical life on local regimental bands. In his thorough and well-documented overview, *Music in Canada 1534–1914*, Helmut Kallmann states that "without doubt the regimental band was the first great musical contribution of Britain to Canada." As Canada's expanding garrison towns eventually became cosmopolitan cities, the regimental bands became far more than just sources of marches and musical accompaniments to ceremonies. Their performances helped foster an appetite for concert music that led to the development of orchestral societies and associations devoted to indoor music-making on both large and small scales.

Toronto, which would welcome the provocative architecture of Roy Thomson Hall in 1982, didn't get its own formal music society until 1845, decades behind other centres, such as Halifax. Still, music had its role in the communal life of early Toronto. In 1794, three years after the city's founding as the Town of York, Elizabeth Simcoe, wife of Lieutenant Governor John Graves Simcoe, recounted in her diary hearing "a band of music stationed near" as she "dined in the woods on Major Shanks' farm lot." Later that same year, she reported having "a large party from the garrison to dinner. A boat with music accompanied them; we heard it in the evening until they had passed the town. It sounds delightfully."

In 1818, Muddy York was home to only one thousand or so inhabitants and, according to the census taker, a single violinist (as Kallmann records). But as the nineteenth century wore on and the town's growth accelerated, choirs, bands, and

orchestras began to develop and present major works. Many of these concerts took place in churches or in places designed for other purposes. It was at Mr. Frank's Assembly Rooms on December 22, 1825, that Toronto's future mayor William Lyon Mackenzie attended his first local theatrical performance, a presentation of Samuel Arnold's opera *The Mountaineers*, performed by a company from Rochester, New York. Toronto's first dedicated theatre, a converted Methodist church renamed the Theatre Royal, did not open until 1834.

By the 1840s and 1850s there were enough auditoriums of sufficient size to make possible visits by some of the greatest artists of the day, including the soprano Adelina Patti, the violinists Ole Bull and Henry Vieuxtemps, and Franz Liszt's well-travelled rival in the art of piano playing, Sigismund Thalberg. Toronto's first permanent secular home for music appeared with the opening of St. Lawrence Hall on King Street East in 1850. It was there, in the second-floor auditorium a year later, that the "Swedish Nightingale," Jenny Lind — who had managed to arrive on the urban shore of Lake Ontario even before the railroad — sang for a capacity audience whose members had paid as much as $3 a ticket.

St. Lawrence Hall, a four-storey neoclassical structure designed by Toronto architect William Thomas, was intended as a multi-purpose building attached by a market annex to City Hall, with shops on the ground floor and offices upstairs. A range of performances, including minstrel shows and Gilbert and Sullivan productions by the students of Upper Canada College, initially kept its doors open, but the arrival of newer, larger, and more conveniently located venues led to its decline as a performance space by the beginning of the twentieth century. The restoration of St. Lawrence Hall in 1967 as a centennial project, and its use for a number of years as rehearsal and office space by the National Ballet of Canada and its current tenants, including Opera Atelier, gave the old hall a new life. Even so, its golden performance years belong to the past.

Touring opera companies passed regularly through Toronto during the second half of the nineteenth century, with performances at one of several theatres, including the Grand Opera House on Adelaide Street West. Its opening in the fall of 1874 was a major development in the cultural life of Toronto, trumpeted on the front cover of the *Canadian Illustrated News*. An issue of the same publication in the following year showed the theatre's interior during a performance of Handel's *Messiah*.

In her pioneering 1985 study *Look at the Record*, Joan Parkhill Baillie celebrated a number of the nineteenth-century venues that have since vanished. They included the hyperbolically designated Royal Opera House, which was a converted carpentry shop on Theatre Lane behind a row of buildings on King Street, to City Hall, where the council of the newly incorporated City of Toronto met in 1834, three years after the building's construction. It was on this same site, following the great fire of April 7, 1849, that the more substantial St. Lawrence Hall and Market were built.

The Grand Opera House — also known as Mrs. Morrison's Opera House, thanks to its manager Charlotte Morrison, a retired actor — eventually drew much of the public's attention away from St. Lawrence Hall. With a seating capacity of 1,323 when it was first built, it offered a commodious auditorium as well as a spacious stage for performers, just the ticket for a town in full expansion.

Like gaslit nineteenth-century theatres before it, and despite being fitted with the latest in fire-prevention equipment, the Grand Opera House was severely damaged by fire five years after its opening, but was back in operation less than two months later — with an increased seating capacity of 1,750. In his 1978 illustrated history, *Lost Toronto*, William Dendy noted that the Grand and Royal Opera Houses were in direct competition with each other until the latter was levelled by fire in early 1883.

Although many an opera was presented on the Grand's stage, including the Savoy operas brought over from London, in practice it was very much a multi-purpose venue. The Grand Opera House was home to an annual ball, during which the orchestra-level seats were covered with a dance floor, and was the site of concerts presented by the Toronto Philharmonic Society following the fire at the Royal. As well, the Grand Opera House hosted the great actors and singers of the day, staging performances by luminaries including Sarah Bernhardt, Sir Henry Irving, Dame Ellen Terry, and Sir Herbert Beerbohm Tree. As popular a draw as it had become during the city's Victorian boom years, the owners had a hard time making any money from it, noted Dendy in a reminder of how uncertain finances in the performing arts have been since the advent of the public auditorium.

"After an illustrious and eventful career," Joan Parkhill Baillie wrote, the Grand Opera House "was finally demolished in 1927 when the days of grand opera houses were believed to be at an end." The only remaining evidence of these heady times is Grand Opera Lane, a tiny street named in its honour.

Meanwhile, several other venues were erected to meet the needs of the growing community. Albert Hall, which opened in 1875 on Yonge Street, was located above a tailor shop and photography salon. Shaftsbury Hall (1877) on Queen Street West was a much larger, 1,700-seat venue sharing accommodations with the YMCA. Richmond Street West had St. Andrew's Hall (1880). Adelaide Street West boasted the short-lived Holman Opera House (1883), better known as a skating rink, and the Toronto Opera House (1886) just a few doors west. At King and York Streets, the Academy of Music (1890) was among Toronto's first public buildings to be lit by electricity; it transformed itself into the Princess Theatre following an 1895 renovation and hosted the Canadian premiere of Richard Wagner's opera *Parsifal* in 1905 and Giacomo Puccini's *Madama Butterfly* two years later.

As this list suggests, Victorian Toronto had a burgeoning arts community entirely in keeping with a population that had grown to 181,200 by 1891. It wasn't until 1894, however, that the city acquired its musical crown jewel: Massey Music Hall. Hart Massey's gift to the city of course by no means ended the construction of performance spaces, for repeated fires and redevelopment forced a nomadic life on the vast majority of Toronto's actors, musicians, and impresarios.

In the early years of the century, Cawthra Mulock, son of the jurist and statesman Sir William Mulock, assembled a group of Toronto businessmen keen to raise the city's cultural profile. They invited architect John M. Lyle to build "the finest theatre on the continent" on King Street West, and if Lyle did not quite succeed in his mission, it can be argued that he came close. The 1,497-seat Royal Alexandra Theatre set a new standard of elegance and comfort for its patrons when it opened its doors in 1907, playing host to operas and operettas as well as theatre and musical comedies. One of its crumbling scrapbooks even contains a yellowing newspaper advertisement for "positively" the final farewell tour of Sarah Bernhardt.

The Royal Alexandra Theatre.

Photo by James Victor Salmon. Courtesy of the Toronto Public Library.

Lyle's facsimile of a London West End playhouse would become the cradle of operatic life in modern-day Toronto. In 1955, the Royal Conservatory Opera Company's three-production opera festival came to be known as the Opera Festival Company, four years later acquiring its present name of the Canadian Opera Company. In 1963, discount department store owner Ed Mirvish saved the Royal Alexandra Theatre from the wrecker's ball, restoring it to its Edwardian glory. Meanwhile, the Canadian Opera Company had moved to a more spacious rental venue in the 3,200-seat O'Keefe Centre, with general director Herman Geiger-Torel admitting that for twelve years his company had "cheated" at the smaller theatre on King Street because its pit could not hold the number of orchestral players its productions required. A number of venues joined the cityscape between the opening nights of the Royal Alex and the O'Keefe, as they were popularly known. A second gift from the Massey family financed the construction of Hart House in 1923 on the campus of the University of Toronto. The main auditorium of Hart House became home to Ernest MacMillan's Conservatory Opera Company. MacMillan himself was at the organ console on March 26, 1931, at the unveiling of the 1,014-seat art deco auditorium on the seventh floor of Eaton's handsome new flagship store at Yonge and College Streets. Soon welcomed as the city's mid-sized alternative to Massey Hall, Eaton Auditorium played host to the first performances of the National Ballet of Canada and a who's who

Ernest MacMillan, former music director and conductor of the Toronto Symphony Orchestra, backstage at Massey Hall with concert master Elie Spivak. Photo by Roseborough & Rice 1946.

Courtesy of the City of Toronto Archives.

of twentieth-century musical artists. It was also Glenn Gould's favourite local recording venue until it was mothballed in 1977. Its resurrection in 2003 as the Carlu (named after the auditorium's French interior designer, Jacques Carlu) was warmly applauded but, because it is a private events facility, public concerts there have been, to quote Sporting Life in *Porgy and Bess*, "a sometime thing."

Like many other cities on New York's Metropolitan Opera North American touring circuit in the 1950s, Toronto could not provide an appropriate venue with sufficient audience capacity to accommodate the continent's foremost purveyor of the art form. Massey Hall had hosted in the 1940s members of the Met with full chorus and orchestra. The Met's visits to Toronto became so popular and so expensive that it had to be moved to Maple Leaf Gardens, as William Kilbourn points out in his centennial history, *Intimate Grandeur: One Hundred Years at Massey Hall*. When Rudolf Bing, the Met's famously crusty general manager, was asked what he thought of the long-time home of the Toronto Maple Leafs, he reportedly responded, doubtless with arched eyebrows, that "it's the best hockey arena we play in."

It was the O'Keefe Centre that served as Toronto's principal home for opera and large travelling shows until the opening in 2006 of the Four Seasons Centre for the Performing Arts. The O'Keefe Centre was launched with celebratory fanfare in October of 1960 with a pre-Broadway run of Lerner and Loewe's *Camelot* starring Richard Burton, Julie Andrews, and former Canadian Opera Company baritone Robert Goulet. The $12-million auditorium was built by Canadian Brewers Ltd. with a then-popular fan-shaped seating layout to a design by Earl C. Morgan. Quickly and with mixed emotions dubbed "the barn that beer built," it was eventually purchased by Toronto's metropolitan government for $2.7 million and has continued to operate, first as the Hummingbird Centre and more recently as the Sony Centre for the Performing Arts.

An auditorium better suited to opera appeared in 1961 with the completion of the MacMillan Theatre in the Edward Johnson Building, the new home for the University of Toronto's Faculty of Music. Designed with a stage as large as that of the O'Keefe Centre's in order to accommodate Canadian Opera Company rehearsals, it boasted decent acoustics but a seat count of only 815, deliberately limiting its commercial potential so that it would be used primarily for the university's purposes. Other academic facilities appeared over the ensuing years, at such institutions as Ryerson Polytechnic Institute (now Ryerson University) and York University. Meanwhile, the city's recital activity, once dependent on the modest likes of Heliconian Hall, built in 1875, became enriched by the St. Lawrence Centre's Jane Mallett Theatre, the George Weston Recital Hall at the Toronto Centre for the Arts, and the Glenn Gould Studio at the Canadian Broadcasting Centre.

Pictured here in 1854, Government House stood on the southwest corner of King and Simcoe Streets, site of the future Roy Thomson Hall. Lithograph by Lucius Richard O'Brien.

Courtesy of the Toronto Public Library.

The Canadian Opera Company finally managed to build its own home, after decades of fits and starts, at the corner of University Avenue and Queen Street West. The 2,071-seat Four Seasons Centre was hailed as "the first building of its kind in Canada." Designed by Jack Diamond (of Diamond Schmitt Architects), the venue was built specifically for the needs of opera and ballet.

Three years later, the Royal Conservatory of Music unveiled the Telus Centre, designed by Marianne McKenna of Toronto's KPMB Architects. Its largest venue, Michael and Sonja Koerner Concert Hall, with seating for 1,135, was quickly called the city's finest recital hall. The acoustician for both the Four Seasons Centre and Koerner Hall was Bob Essert of Sound Space Design.

Different in scale and scope, Roy Thomson Hall and Koerner Hall may overlap in some respects, but they have come to complement each other, as programming has adjusted to focus on respective competitive advantages. Roy Thomson Hall seats 2,630 and presents superstar attractions and large ensembles, while Koerner Hall caters more to recitals and chamber music.

Like all major cities, Toronto now welcomes a range of musical offerings and venues. Where once was a vast and harsh land defined by its insular garrisons, there is now a burgeoning cultural landscape that welcomes international artists and international audiences.

Photo by Brent Kitagawa.

CHAPTER 1

The Grand Old Lady of Shuter Street

THE MASSEYS ARE among the great Canadian families, with a governor general (Vincent) and a distinguished film actor (Raymond) among their better-known progeny. Less well known than either of these men is their grandfather, Hart, who parlayed his father's Newcastle foundry into one of the continent's foremost farm implement manufacturers, and became in the process one of Toronto's leading philanthropists. Along with the Fred Victor Mission and a number of church charities, Hart bankrolled the construction of what would come to be known as Massey Music Hall, one of North America's finest nineteenth-century venues for what H.L. Mencken called "the tone art." The building cost just in excess of $150,000 and Hart Massey offered it as a magnanimous gift to the City of Toronto, named to honour his son Charles Albert Massey, who had died during a typhus epidemic in 1884 at the age of 36.

Until the 1920s, Massey Hall was said to be the only place of its kind in Canada, designed primarily for the presentation of musical performances.

Plaque honouring Charles A. Massey in the lobby of Massey Hall.

Photo by Alexandra Basen.

With its cramped site and unprepossessing brick facade — more handsome but costlier stone had been proposed but was ultimately rejected — architect Sidney R. Badgley's landmark edifice hardly invited an aesthetic comparison with New York's Carnegie Hall, Boston's Symphony Hall, or Cincinnati's Music Hall, all of which were built within a couple of decades of each other. Toronto's was a utilitarian structure. When the Historic Sites and Monuments Board of Canada ornamented the facade to mark the centennial of Massey Hall with a commemorative plaque, the inscription read, in part: "Although criticized for its plain exterior, the concert hall has earned widespread renown for its outstanding acoustics."

Those acoustics were put to a dramatic test in April 1961 when one of Europe's noted physicists, Professor Fritz Winckel of Berlin, pulled out a .38-calibre revolver and fired a blank cartridge toward its ceiling arches. Consulting his stopwatch to assess the reverberation time, he proclaimed Toronto's major concert hall one of the finest in the world. Though this single-shot diagnosis makes for a good story, Winkel's declamation was based on more than mere gunplay. He had taken measurements and listened to the Toronto Symphony Orchestra in rehearsal, finding more than a few reasons to share the enthusiasm for the place expressed by his friend, the Berlin Philharmonic Orchestra's celebrated post–Second World War conductor Herbert von Karajan.

The interior of Massey Hall as it was in the late 1890s.

Courtesy of the Ontario Archives.

Light (and noise) flooded into Massey Hall through the original stained glass windows.

Courtesy of the National Archives of Canada.

In *Intimate Grandeur*, William Kilbourn details the sheer improbability of Hart Massey's enterprise, characterizing the Toronto of 1894 as "a provincial, Protestant, philistine city of 180,000 inhabitants," and Massey himself as "a tight-fisted, quarrelsome, opinionated old autocrat." But the fearsome disposition was offset by a philanthropic bent that Kilbourn roots in Hart Massey's Methodist upbringing. Whatever the explanation, on a sunny mid-June evening in 1894, he and his carriage-driven family joined Governor General Sir John Campbell Hamilton Gordon, Earl of Aberdeen, along with anyone else fortunate enough to procure one of the 3,500 available seats, to face an orchestra and choir of 750 voices performing Handel's *Messiah* at Massey Hall's grand opening.

Frederick Torrington, the conductor of that first performance, can be seen to this very day gazing from a framed portrait in the Gerstein Library of the University of Toronto's Medical Sciences Building. The acknowledged leader of the city's classical-music community in the late nineteenth century, Torrington contributed mightily to Toronto's reputation as a city of choirs. The red-brick building at the corner of Shuter and Victoria Streets soon became the prized destination of the most ambitious among them.

Architect Sidney R. Badgley was not without credentials for serving Torrington's ambitions for music in Toronto. A Canadian based in Cleveland, he was the designer of a number of auditorium-style Methodist churches. His initial plans for Massey Music Hall, as it was called before its name change in 1933, included a setback from Shuter Street and the incorporation of ground-floor shops to flank the main entrance. Unfortunately for Badgley's plans, Hart Massey refused to pay the requested price for the lot to the south of the present site. Torrington's desire for a shoebox shape characteristic of some of Europe's finest homes for music had to be modified in favour of Badgley's preference for a squared space with curved, horseshoe-shaped galleries, reminiscent of his church designs.

In its present well-worn state, it is less easy to appreciate the extravagant Moorish features Badgley envisaged for the hall's scalloped interior, with its multicoloured decorative details and its art nouveau stained glass windows. The windows still exist, and although a few have been revealed in recent years, most still await their rediscovery behind coverings installed over the decades to mask the noises of an increasingly motorized and congested urban core. In an interesting week from the hall's later history, adjoining streets had to be temporarily closed off by special permission of Toronto's mayor when Igor Stravinsky came to town to record some of his music with Elmer Iseler's Festival Singers for CBS Records. Sound isolation, a necessary and expensive feature of modern concert hall construction, barely concerned architects during the days of horse-drawn buggies.

A strict moralist who disliked the theatre almost as much as he disliked alcohol, Hart Massey never anticipated the range of activities his civic gift would eventually accommodate. Despite its lack of theatrical wings or fly space, short decades after its founder's demise Massey Hall was welcoming visiting vaudeville acts, the ballet troupe of Anna Pavlova, and even the famed boxer Jack Dempsey. If Badgley had a crystal ball with which to peer into Massey Hall's future uses, or had he been given more space to design the hall as he had imagined, then he might have better accommodated people on both sides of the (occasionally present) footlights. Lobbies were cramped and dressing rooms minimal, and the fact that about 4,400 people (counting performers and staff as well as audience members) managed to squeeze into the building on opening night, June 14, 1894, still amazes a twenty-first-century observer.

Hart Massey did not long survive the triumph of opening night. Unwell even at the time of Massey Music Hall's public debut, he died on February 20, 1896. The lights in the Massey family box suddenly went out that evening during a performance of Haydn's *The Creation*. At its end, Frederick Torrington, who understood what had happened, turned to the audience to make an announcement. As everyone stood in silence, the orchestra brought the evening to its sad conclusion, playing the "Dead March" from Handel's *Saul*.

Although the years ahead witnessed financial ups and downs, the hall's trustees strove to meet the conditions of Hart Massey's deed of gift: to make the hall available for the "musical, educational, and industrial advancement of the people, the cultivation of good citizenship and patriotism, the promotion of philanthropy,

The original Massey Hall
stage and private boxes.

Photo by B.W. Kilburn, 1894.
Courtesy of the Toronto Public
Library.

religion and temperance, and for holding meetings and entertainments consistent
with any of the above purposes." Orchestras arrived from Buffalo and Chicago;
the noted evangelist Dwight Moody held revival meetings. Even Lady Aberdeen
descended from the box she had shared with her husband on opening night to
lecture on "The Present Irish Literary Revival." A full day's rent of $90 in summer
and $110 in winter made it a less costly venue than many of its American
counterparts. On the other hand, a depressed economy discouraged higher rents
and there was no civic subsidy to cover deficits. It did not take long for the trustees
to realize the importance of drumming up rental business.

The hall's management went into partnership with a succession of presenters,
as early as 1901 expanding their vision for the hall to include the sinful art form
known as opera in order to entertain the Duke of Cornwall and York and his
consort (the future King George V and Queen Mary). Aside from taking out a
couple of rows of seats to accommodate an improvised orchestra pit, there was

little the hall's management could do to disguise its unsuitability as an opera house. Even so, in part because of its large capacity, it became one of Toronto's preferred operatic venues during its first half-century, with the touring San Carlo Opera crowding the likes of Gaetano Donizetti's *Lucia di Lammermoor* and even Giuseppe Verdi's grandiose *Aida* onto its concert-scaled stage.

Massey Hall's suitability as a home for large-scale choral performances was established on opening night, so there was little surprise when, in 1894, the newly formed Toronto Mendelssohn Choir took up residence under the direction of its Elmira-born, Boston- and Leipzig-trained founding maestro, Augustus Vogt. Such was Vogt's early success in setting a high standard for his choir that it soon found itself collaborating with orchestras from Pittsburgh and Chicago and receiving rave reviews for its appearances at Carnegie Hall. *Musical America* even stated that "the Mendelssohn Choir represents in the realm of choral music what the Boston Symphony stands for in its domain."

Although Massey Hall and its resident choir were highly regarded, bills still had to be paid and that meant appealing to a broader public than admirers of choral music in general and Felix Mendelssohn in particular. There were limits, however. After Isadora Duncan, the high priestess of modern dance, performed barefoot in 1909, negotiations were cancelled with the next modern dance ensemble exercising such cavalier disdain for the local audience's penchant for modestly attired performers. It seemed somehow less déclassé when the Scottish singer-comedian Harry Lauder arrived a few years later with his "amazing, football-playing dogs." And there was apparently no significant objection, in less enlightened times, to Jacob Adler portraying Shylock in *The Merchant of Venice* in Yiddish. Massey Hall

Massey Hall, 1914.

Courtesy of the Toronto Reference Library.

even anticipated Roy Thomson Hall's future role as a part-time movie theatre, with runs of D.W. Griffiths's *Birth of a Nation* and *Intolerance* packing the galleries. The music hall had become home to a wide range of community activities, from religious services and gatherings of Boy Scouts to a brief stop, courtesy of Eaton's department store, of a red-suited gentleman bearing gifts.

Community events notwithstanding, Massey Hall was Toronto's prestige public venue. The tumultuously welcomed Prince of Wales, the future Edward VIII, spoke there during his November 1919 visit. Less than a year later, no less an amateur pianist than Lady Eaton accompanied the Guelph-born Edward Johnson in a charity song recital — Sir John Eaton ordered the stage specially scrubbed for the occasion and filled with potted flowers and plants from the family estate. A whole roster of celebrity speakers followed, ranging from the controversial philosopher Bertrand Russell to Howard Carter, the archaeologist who discovered King Tut's tomb.

The first Toronto Symphony Orchestra was born in 1908 out of an ensemble organized by Toronto Conservatory of Music director Dr. Edward Fisher and led by pianist/conductor Frank Welsman. The financial and manpower demands of the First World War eroded support for the ensemble, which disbanded in the summer of 1918. By 1923, mainly thanks to the efforts of violinist/conductor Luigi von Kunitz, Massey Hall once again became Toronto's regular home for symphonic music. Initially known as the New Symphony Orchestra, the eventually renamed Toronto Symphony Orchestra offered twilight concerts at first so its players could dash off for the pits of the city's numerous vaudeville and movie houses, which paid better and more frequently than the classical orchestra's less frequent concerts. Under music director von Kunitz and his successor Ernest MacMillan — who would later become the first musician from the British Empire to earn a knighthood — the Toronto Symphony Orchestra's concerts multiplied and its season lengthened. The hall had become a home (or at least landlord) to one of North America's major orchestral ensembles.

It is sometimes forgotten that this important role did not prevent Vincent Massey and some of his fellow trustees from considering the hall rundown, outdated, and possibly in need of replacement by the late 1920s. The Great Depression, the popularity of radio, and the arrival of sound films nixed that notion in favour of a substantial renovation in 1933. The number of seats was reduced from 3,500 to 2,765 and the lobby spaces were expanded, with the Massey family once again subsidizing the cost. Vincent Massey had even accepted the presidency of the board of the Toronto Symphony Orchestra.

Although the TSO was claiming a greater number of evenings per year on stage at Massey Hall, there remained as late as 1948 the need to rent the hall for additional events to pay the bills. Perhaps the most surprising of these were the boxing and wrestling matches fought on stage, including a 1919 bout featuring

The Toronto Symphony Orchestra plays Massey Hall, 1926.

Photo by Brightling. Courtesy of the Toronto Public Library.

future heavyweight champion of the world Jack Dempsey. Notable visitors of a more artistic bent included George Gershwin, playing his *Rhapsody in Blue*, and the ambitious Toronto director/playwright Herman Voaden, staging T.S. Eliot's new verse play *Murder in the Cathedral*, with music by the city's foremost composer, Healey Willan, sung by his own Church of St. Mary Magdalene Choir.

William Kilbourn describes the quarter-century from 1931 to 1956 as "Massey Hall's golden age," with the Toronto Symphony Orchestra under Ernest MacMillan and the Toronto Mendelssohn Choir enjoying pride of place. The 1960s and 1970s told a different tale, with the arrival of new venues around the city, and with Massey Hall's continuing physical decline leading to renewed calls for the construction of a new building. The primitive nature of the hall's heating and ventilation systems, for example, was made clear in 1977 when Vladimir Horowitz demanded a constant 20-degree Celsius temperature for the stability of his beloved Steinway grand. The hall's dedicated veteran manager Joe Cartan had to devote the better part of his day to monitoring the temperature. Cartan, who worked at the hall from 1929 until his retirement in 1984, did more than just manage the heating and cooling systems — he kept the entire venue running on a shoestring budget.

The hall's management had tried to address some of the ongoing problems in terms of audience and performer comfort by installing new seats and the second-floor lounge. And changes to fire codes meant that the wooden floor on the orchestra level had to be torn up and replaced with concrete. There are people who still speak sadly of the acoustical changes produced by inserting concrete beneath the stage.

Eaton Auditorium had become the favourite venue for ballet, and many concert presenters also turned to other venues. Taking the place of more traditional shows, Charlie Parker arrived at Massey Hall in May of 1953 with Dizzy Gillespie, Charles

Mingus, Bud Powell, and Max Roach to perform what has gone down in jazz lore as one of the finest concerts of its kind of all time. It took the move of the Toronto Symphony Orchestra to Roy Thomson Hall in 1982 for a definitive change in profile to take place, with jazz, country, and rock music replacing many of the dates vacated by Ludwig van Beethoven and Johannes Brahms. Massey Hall became folksinger Gordon Lightfoot's signature venue. Dolly Parton chose it as the site of her Toronto debut. And Bob Dylan created a sensation in 1965 by joining his Canadian backup group, The Band, in going electric for the second half of his program.

Depending on one's perspective, the story of Roy Thomson Hall can be said to have begun either in the 1920s, when the trustees of Massey Hall began to consider retiring the Grand Old Lady of Shuter Street, or in 1965, when orchestra president Edward Pickering heard the Toronto Symphony Orchestra rehearsing on tour in the United Kingdom. In the first instance, acoustics were not the main issue. In the second, they were. A nineteenth-century hall inevitably calls for occasional renovation, if not replacement; in Massey Hall's case the trustees initially opted for refurbishment. Yet even with its expanded lobbies and new seats, by the 1960s the hall had acquired a growing chorus of acoustical critics, many of them from the ranks of the Toronto Symphony Orchestra.

It was those voices that orchestra president Edward Pickering heard in other concert halls, declaring how much easier it was for the players to hear each other onstage than it was for them to do so back home. It wasn't Pickering's only exposure to such comments. Although he was a well-informed businessman rather than a professional musician, Pickering had personally witnessed the difficulties

Toronto Symphony Orchestra general manager Walter Homburger, music director Seiji Ozawa, and trombonist Murray Ginsberg leave for a European tour, 1965.

Photo by Frank Grant. City of Toronto Archives, Fonds 329, Series 1569, File 1522, Item 1.

Seiji Ozawa, the orchestra's young Japanese conductor, had experienced while working with the orchestra, including an inability to hear certain sections properly. Pickering was of course also aware of the cramped conditions backstage and the fact that neither players nor listeners had much to be thankful for in the hall's current state, beyond the justly admired warmth of its sound.

When the Toronto Symphony Orchestra returned from this particular tour of Great Britain, having been praised in the London *Sunday Times* following its Royal Festival Hall concert for delivering orchestral playing of "great international class," the chorus for a new venue reached a new crescendo. In October of 1966, Pickering joined Massey Hall's board chair Hugh Lawson in announcing the intention to build a new concert hall.

The decision to build a new hall was supported by a report commissioned from William Severns. The former managing director of the Los Angeles Philharmonic recommended, as TSO managing director Walter Homburger later recalled, "that a committee be set up to study our requirements for a new hall and ways and means to bring this about." This committee was established jointly by the boards of the hall and orchestra and also involved representatives from the Toronto Mendelssohn Choir. In a 1983 speech to the Rotary Club of Toronto, Pickering recalled that the committee "visited most of the concert halls built in North America since the war," and that "by 1972 we had developed guidelines as to our acoustical and architectural objectives."

With all the history Massey Hall embodied, leaving it would not be any easier for the TSO than it had been years earlier when the New York Philharmonic left Carnegie Hall for a new home at Lincoln Center for the Performing Arts. As in

This Toronto Historical Board plaque celebrates Massey Music Hall.

midtown Manhattan, practicality trumped sentimentality. In 1967, the Massey Hall Board of Trustees declared that there would be a new hall on a new site.

Where did that leave Massey Hall? To raise the millions of dollars necessary to realize their objective, some committee members, Pickering among them, believed they might have to sell the existing site for redevelopment. When news of this possibility became public knowledge, the reaction from many Torontonians was swift and decisive: there was no way that eighty years of the city's cultural history could be sacrificed to an uncertain future. We have to remember that this was the same period when the now-defunct Eaton's department store chain was planning to build its new corporate offices and flagship retail location as anchors of a massive modern shopping centre that would completely change the face and feel of a long block of Yonge Street between Dundas and Queen Streets. A group of activists began to lobby for Massey Hall. Sam Sniderman, known to record buyers of the day as Sam the Record Man, offered to take over the old venue. Although the offer made newspaper headlines, it made no headway with Massey Hall's board. Luckily for posterity, the Grand Old Lady still had a place in the city's affections. In New York, a last-minute campaign led by violinist Isaac Stern had saved Carnegie Hall from demolition. With the memory of this incident fresh in people's minds, the wrecking ball didn't even come close.

The Toronto Symphony Orchestra's final performance at Massey Hall took place on June 4, 1982. Despite the loss of the building's primary tenant, rentals kept coming in and bills continued to be paid. Kilbourn records that by the 1990s, rental fees ranged from $1,000 to $10,000 a night, depending on the ticket prices, and breaking even would normally require selling 1,500 seats at $20 each. The addition of air

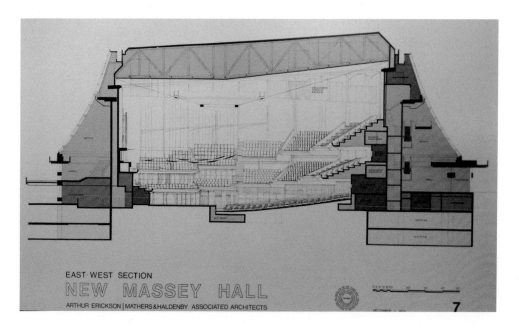

EAST-WEST SECTION
NEW MASSEY HALL
ARTHUR ERICKSON | MATHERS & HALDENBY ASSOCIATED ARCHITECTS   7

Drawing of New Massey Hall by Arthur Erickson and Mathers & Haldenby.

Edward A. Pickering, President,
and the Board of Governors of
Massey Hall
cordially invite you to attend
the unveiling of the architects' models for
New Massey Hall
Thursday, September 8, 1977
11:00 a.m.
City Hall Council Chamber
Toronto

An invitation to see the architects' models of New Massey Hall.

conditioning in 1989, prompted by a seven-month run of the Andrew Lloyd Webber musical *Cats*, made it possible for an audience to stay comfortable inside even during the hottest months. In the 1990s, despite the arrival of Roy Thomson Hall and the Toronto Centre for the Arts across from the North York Civic Centre, the Canadian music industry still voted Massey Hall Canada's "best music venue over 1,500 seats."

Industry and audience accolades notwithstanding, the Corporation of Massey Hall and Roy Thomson Hall recognized the inevitability of a major renovation. Several decades ago, the owners of a similar nineteenth-century concert hall, Philadelphia's Academy of Music, faced the same inevitability when a chunk of its stage ceiling fell down, nearly knighting conductor Leopold Stokowski! Whether or not the news penetrated Toronto ears, today's visitors to the Grand Old Lady of Shuter Street need only look upward to notice the temporary insurance taken out on her overhead plasterwork in the form of protective wire mesh. Performers and listeners alike look forward to the day when concerts can once again take place on her storied stage without the need of such safety precautions.

CHAPTER 2

A Child of Perseverance

TWO FACTORS DETERMINED whether the project for New Massey Hall (as Roy Thomson Hall was then known) would attract popular support: the right site and the right design. Both took some time to be realized, but the planning, waiting, and overcoming of unforeseen roadblocks were all accomplished in due course.

When Edward Pickering and his building committee failed to secure their preferred location, a vacant property southeast of King and Church Streets, they considered two other parcels of land: one at the corner of Bay and Gerrard Streets, and the other at Harbourfront, but both were rejected as too difficult to access via public transportation. They then approached the City of Toronto for help. Luckily, this move coincided with the city's negotiations with the Canadian National and Canadian Pacific Railroads regarding the redevelopment of a large parcel of railway property on the western fringe of the downtown core into Metro Centre, the future seat of Toronto's regional administration. By 1971, after two years of intensive lobbying and the help of some key aldermen, space for the new hall was made available as part of an agreement between the city and the railways. Was this the end of the story? Not quite.

The initial Metro Centre project collapsed. A revived plan was brokered through Marathon Realty, Canadian Pacific's real estate division, with the help of Mayor David Crombie. In this second plan, city council decreed that there must be a residential component in the development, but Marathon, a commercial operator, wasn't interested in getting involved in residential real estate. It wasn't until

In 1972, Douglas Haldenby (left) and Arthur Erickson were invited to form a joint architectural venture, with the design of the hall going to Erickson and the technical and administrative role to Haldenby.

Courtesy of Shin Sugino.

1976 that the mayor and Marathon Realty finally came to an agreement, making a site at the southwest corner of King and Simcoe Streets available to the new hall on advantageous terms. Even then, there was another hurdle. The Toronto Historical Board demanded the incorporation of an old Canadian Pacific Express building and freight sheds into the design of the new edifice and had to be convinced that these structures were incompatible with the look and needs of a modern concert hall. Formal approval of the project finally came in November of that year.

During all this jockeying, preparatory work on a design for the hall was already underway. The mission statement issued by the building committee was ambitious:

> Our prime purpose is to carry forward to the new building the tradition of Massey Hall as one of the world's finest concert halls and to create the finest concert hall, old or new, anywhere

in the world. There should be something inspiring and soaring, indeed a lyrical quality about the structure, as befitting the glories of the sounds that await within.

The choice of architect, the culmination of years of research, and careful consideration of more than a dozen detailed presentations promised great things.

As the *Canadian Encyclopedia* points out, Vancouver-born Arthur Erickson was "perhaps the first Canadian architect to be widely known by the international public." Highly praised for his designs for the University of Lethbridge, Simon Fraser University, the Museum of Anthropology at the University of British Columbia, and the Canadian Pavilion at Expo '70 in Osaka, he had become known for creating "buildings integral to the landscapes in which they are placed." Because New Massey Hall was initially placed in the context of a larger development known as Downtown West, Erickson drafted designs that would allow his firm to take charge of the whole project. The architect's vision for a new hub for Toronto's downtown rose around a large, water-filled public square. But, as is so often the case when big ideas meet economic realities, Erickson did not get the opportunity to build Downtown West or see the realization of New Massey Hall as he had originally envisioned it.

The choice of Erickson as architect reflected the high level of ambition embodied in the project. So did the choice of Theodore Schultz as acoustician and the freedom he was given. A physicist, Schultz belonged to Bolt, Beranek and Newman,

Left to right: Edmund Bovey, Edward Pickering, and Theodore Schultz at an acoustical test by the Toronto Symphony Orchestra in Roy Thomson Hall.

Courtesy of the TSO.

a group of acoustical experts based in the Boston area. The firm, now known as Raytheon BBN Technologies, had presided over the widely criticized acoustical design of Philharmonic Hall (renamed Avery Fisher Hall in 1973), which opened in 1962 at New York's Lincoln Center. At the time of the building committee's decision, Pickering explained that Schultz's poor result had been "mainly due to the fact that the acoustician had no freedom of action." He didn't attribute any failings to the firm itself. And, to make sure that Schultz's expertise would prevail, Pickering explained that he and the committee had "informed the architects that the acoustical expert would have senior ranking and be responsible for determining the size of the auditorium, its configuration, materials and all other matters having a bearing on sound." According to Pickering's accounts to the press and speeches made at the time the hall was being built, Schultz met more frequently with the building committee than did Erickson, and he was given "everything he said he needed."

If this approach sounds idealistic, it was also novel. Usually, in projects like these, acoustical consultants reported to the architect, who felt free to accept or ignore their recommendations. The experience at Lincoln Center's Philharmonic Hall helped change that practice, and Roy Thomson Hall led the way — or at least tried to.

Despite a clean-slate approach on the part of the building committee, the new hall's future users did not give architect or acoustician total control; they had their own list of needs and wants. Massey Hall sat 2,765 people, and Toronto Symphony Orchestra managing director Walter Homburger made it clear that, with a growing audience to accommodate, the orchestra wanted a venue with three thousand seats. It seemed a reasonable request given how, at the time, the TSO enjoyed the highest number of subscribers of any orchestra in North America. Against this demand, the board wanted to preserve the relative intimacy of the old hall and give everyone a clear view, which militated against using the classic shoebox shape of many of Europe's most highly regarded venues. While admitting that "it is of course much easier to get good sound in a small hall seating say 2,000 persons than in a large one," Pickering added that "the trouble with the smaller size is that a major orchestra cannot make ends meet playing to a small house." The economics of the situation required compromise.

If it is beginning to sound as if the planners of New Massey Hall were talking themselves into believing they could have it both ways — to be big and still be the best — then that is what the evidence suggests. Pure concert halls were a relative rarity in North America, and the two halls most similar to the project were flourishing. In Canada, few would have argued against the economic viability of the 2,990-seat Salle Wilfrid-Pelletier at the Place des Arts to accommodate the Montreal Symphony Orchestra. In the fall of 1966, the new Metropolitan Opera House had opened with an enormous 3,800-seat capacity and better sound than anyone had a right to anticipate.

Model of the building
with Erickson's design for
Downtown West in the
background.

Courtesy of Keith Loffler.

Massey Hall had always paid its own way, and the new hall was expected to do likewise. In the campaign to raise money for the building, the board had promised not to return to governmental and corporate investors for operating subsidies. This already represented the costliest project in the history of the performing arts in Canada, and no one wanted to pay for deficits. Recognizing the challenge they faced, the board sent two of its members, Edmund Bovey and Arnold Edinborough, off to visit a number of American halls to determine what had to be done to assure self-sufficiency. They returned persuaded that rentals from the Toronto Symphony Orchestra, the Toronto Mendelssohn Choir, and other presenters would not pay all the bills and that the new hall would have to do what Massey Hall did in the early decades of its history: become its own impresario. However, the immediate task at hand was not presenting concerts, but getting the city's new venue built to a budget.

Massey Hall's architect had hoped his building could be clad in stone, but had to settle for brick. Arthur Erickson's fate was no different nearly a century later. The acres of complex-shaped glass canopies and tonnes of marble panels looked stunning in renderings, but the expense of turning them into reality would prove prohibitive. Architect Keith Loffler, who was general manager of Erickson's Toronto office, recalls that, in the mid-1970s, there was no glass manufacturer in North America able to create the sort of glass panels the building's canopy would need. What could be produced would cost approximately $5 million more than a conventional roof system. The true cost of architectural innovation really hit home when the final estimates came in from Eastern Construction just before

Christmas 1976, showing projected construction expenses at twice the original estimates. "It is normal for projects to be over budget," Loffler recalled, "but 100 percent over budget is highly unusual." In crisis mode, Erickson put Loffler in charge of the New Massey Hall project, with the express purpose of slashing costs. "The auditorium was sacrosanct," Loffler remembers, "but out of a total budget of $22 to $23 million, the auditorium itself came to $16 or $17 million."

The architects and building committee eliminated a 750-seat combination rehearsal and recital hall as well as a circular reception hall that had been intended for the space now occupied by the surface parking lot on the south side of Roy Thomson Hall. "But this was just a drop in the bucket compared to what we had to save," remembers Loffler. All the parties involved laboured hard over the next six months to identify cuts and come up with solutions, evolving the project from the original plan, known internally as Scheme A, to Scheme O. "When we got to Scheme O, we still weren't on budget and at that point it was recognized that we had skimmed as much as we could," Loffler recalls. The board approved Scheme O, which had reduced the size of the parking garage and had also discarded the north courtyard along King Street, in the hopes that the additional funds needed to complete the project could be raised once construction was underway. At long last, Lieutenant Governor Pauline McGibbon was able to turn the first pile of dirt at a groundbreaking ceremony in September 1978.

Construction begins.

Courtesy of Eastern Construction.

NEW MASSEY HALL
Eastern Construction Co. Ltd.
Date 14 MAY 80 View

The inner and exterior shells — which shield performers and audiences from all external noise — take shape. As Arthur Erickson said, "The whole hall is a shell within a shell; two completely independent concrete shells not even joined over one structure, with eight or ten feet between them, to keep all sound out."

Courtesy of Eastern Construction.

"There must be a moral in all this," mused Pickering in a 1983 address to the Toronto Rotary Club. "Any organization seeking to build a facility of this kind must be prepared to overcome reverses and delays which are not for the faint-hearted." These words turned out to be prophetic for anyone involved in the surge of cultural building projects in Toronto a generation later, especially at the Royal Ontario Museum, the Art Gallery of Ontario, the Royal Conservatory of Music's Telus Centre, and the oft-delayed opera house that would become the Four Seasons Centre for the Performing Arts.

It wasn't just the Massey Hall board's perseverance in the face of multiple obstacles over more than a decade that inspired future cultural dreamers. The way in which the project was funded would also become a model for others across Canada.

All levels of government provided funding toward the building campaign, with Ottawa making the initial $9.4-million commitment in 1972. By the time Roy Thomson Hall opened its doors, the board had raised a total of $44 million, which included $13.3 million from the province of Ontario (drawn from a cultural investment pool fed by Wintario lottery and gaming revenue) and $5 million from the regional government of Metropolitan Toronto, thanks to the unflagging support of Metro Toronto chairman Paul Godfrey. The $16.4 million raised from corporations, foundations, and individuals made this a pioneering venture, since this was

The corner of King and Simcoe Streets was a very active construction site.

Courtesy of Eastern Construction.

the largest amount of money that had ever been raised from the private sector in Canada for a cultural project. Even more significantly, much of the day-to-day fundraising was accomplished by volunteers, not paid professionals.

A veritable who's who of Canadians came together to champion the New Massey Hall Fund in 1978 and the years that followed. The honorary chairmen were Prime Minister Pierre Elliott Trudeau, Premier William Davis, Metro Toronto chairman Paul Godfrey, and Toronto mayor David Crombie, fresh from coaxing fractious municipal councillors into supporting the building of a flagship performance venue. The campaign

The exterior wall takes shape, one piece at a time.

Courtesy of Mackenzie Limited Photography.

Touring the building site: (left to right) project manager James Webster, Edward Pickering, Arnold Edinborough, Nancy Westaway, William Elliott of Eastern Construction, and project administrator Gene Blaine.

Photo by Tony Mihok, *Business Journal*.

co-chairs were W.D.H. Gardiner, deputy chair of the Royal Bank of Canada, and Wood Gundy president C. Edward Medland. The campaign committee was an extraordinary group of Canadian business leaders, many of whom had recently retired from positions of responsibility — grey power in its finest hour.

Former external affairs minister Mitchell Sharp, an amateur pianist who had once played in Massey Hall, volunteered to make the rounds of diplomatic missions, consulates, and embassies to seek international support for the project. In an intriguing twist on development, he sought donations of materials — marble from Italy, hardwood from Germany, mirrors for the giant reflective surfaces in the hall's lobby from Japan, and acres of carpeting from China. He didn't succeed with most of his inquiries, but the scope of his lobbying demonstrated the status of New Massey Hall in our national consciousness.

While high-level gestures may have been good for grabbing headlines, it was a grassroots campaign to endow seats at New Massey Hall for $1,000 each, led by volunteer Judy Simmonds, that cemented the connection between the future building and its surrounding community. As was the case with so many facets of this project, the impetus came from Pickering. "It astounds me when people talk of the concert-going public in terms of black ties and dinner jackets," he told the *Toronto Star* a few months after launching the New Massey Hall Fund. "It's a myth that only the elite are interested in good music and good theatre. There are more subscribers to the Toronto Symphony Orchestra than there are to the Toronto Maple Leafs. We aren't building a hall for the elite, we're building a hall for the people of our community."

Simmonds and her team of volunteers were able to secure endowments for 1,900 seats out of the 2,500 eligible places by the time the venue opened its doors in 1982. The program, completed by the Roy Thomson Hall volunteer committee after the building opened, resulted in a sea of commemorative plaques for donors who came from across Canada, as well as the United States, the United Kingdom, Europe, and the Caribbean. Most seats were named in memory or honour of individuals, including a sixteen-year-old girl who was given a seat by her grandmother. Other places were marked by fans of well-known names in Canadian entertainment, including those of Anne Murray, Gordon Lightfoot, Oscar Peterson, Maureen Forrester, Paul Anka, Tommy Hunter, and the Canadian Brass. A few months before the hall opened, Simmonds announced that $63,000 had been raised for an entire row of seats dedicated to the memory of singer Paul Robeson. He "stood for the freedom and dignity of all the world's peoples and the Paul Robeson Row is one small way of recognizing his numerous contributions particularly in music and the arts," Simmonds announced. To prevent any jockeying for position inside the hall, seat endowments were allocated by lottery.

The campaign's secret weapon was Simmonds herself, branded by the *Toronto Star* in 1982 as "Metro's $2 million woman." She would visit schools and community centres with a ukulele, accompanying herself in a song she had written, "Help Build Roy Thomson Hall, Folks," which she set to the tune of "Take Me Out to the Ballgame." Simmonds's unflagging enthusiasm unleashed a flood of donations raised by individual parents and their children. A bulletin typical of school messages from across the Greater Toronto Area in early 1982 read:

> Ask your children about the presentation by Mrs. Simmons [sic] and get involved with this project. By having a plaque on the back of a seat in Toronto's newest and more modern music hall, memories of Bayview Junior High School will be perpetuated for the lifetime of your child and he/she will feel a part of the on-going cultural development of our community. This is a world-class act. On the average, we would need to raise approximately three dollars per child in order to meet the cost of endowing one seat.

Although building a new performance venue was a mammoth task, no idea, challenge, or donation was too small to make a significant contribution. In the end, Pickering could only describe his tireless board as "a dedicated and selfless group of men and women who have given immensely of time and talent, energy and money. For ability and service, I know of no like body anywhere."

Unfortunately, in an unexpected echo of the hurdles that the advocates for New Massey Hall faced in initial planning stages, the crowning flourish in the capital campaign nearly turned into a fiasco.

Less than a year before the nearly completed building was to open, Kenneth Thomson, owner of the *Globe and Mail* and many other media holdings around the world, offered on behalf of the Thomson family an unconditional gift of $4.5 million — more than a quarter of the private monies needed to cover building costs. The funds were being offered in memory of his father, Roy Thomson, First Baron Thomson of Fleet. This was the largest single donation toward a performing arts project in Canadian history. Thomson wrote to Edward Pickering on December 22, 1981:

> As you know, my father, Roy Herbert Thomson, died in 1976. Following his death his family has been searching for a suitable way to honour his memory and at the same time assist in a worthwhile community project. We can think of nothing more appropriate than the splendid concert hall which you and your Board are erecting at the corner of King & Simcoe Streets in Toronto.

The donation was sufficient to seed a capital fund that would allow the new venue to present emerging Canadian talent on its stage. In appreciation, the board unanimously voted to name New Massey Hall in the late peer's honour, setting off

Proud son: Ken Thomson holds a *Toronto Star* photo of Roy Thomson Hall.

Mike Slaughter / GetStock.com.

a flurry of outrage that taxpayer and community-raised funds had taken a back-row seat to a single private donation.

The fuss came to a head on March 9, 1982, when the City of Toronto Neighbourhoods Committee voted 9–2 to recommend that City Council ask the board to change the name of the new venue to Toronto Concert Hall. The attack was led by Councillor Richard Gilbert, who told the *Globe and Mail* that he realized the city had no direct say in the matter, "but it's the only way that the many people in this city who feel burned by the board's choice can express their feelings." Michael Lyons of the Labour Council of Metro Toronto echoed Gilbert's sentiments more directly, telling the newspaper, "I don't think Ken Thomson should expect the citizens of Metro Toronto to put up millions of dollars to pay for a memorial to his father."

Fortunately, city council realized that this was not their issue to address, Pickering and the board stuck to their plan, the furor dissipated well before opening day in September — and the Thomson family was able to enjoy countless performances and receptions in the new building, as well as a warm relationship with the venue's staff.

Once it had become clear that the public monies were in place and that the capital campaign had made a strong start, Pickering and the board moved swiftly with construction plans in 1977, aiming for a completed building in 1980. Although the shell and some satellite features of Roy Thomson Hall had been changed, there were to be no compromises for the interior of this world-class performance space.

In order to get there, Erickson and Schultz had to juggle multiple expectations governing the size and shape of the facility. The Toronto Symphony Orchestra didn't want to lose a single subscriber. Elmer Iseler wanted sufficient choir seating to accommodate the 150-plus members of the Toronto Mendelssohn Choir. Having visited Royal Festival Hall in London, a number of TSO players even lobbied for a backstage bar. And then there was the issue of acoustics.

Schultz brought to the table his own theories regarding the way people perceive sound in a concert hall. To the acoustician and his colleagues at Bolt, Beranek and Newman, new halls represented an opportunity to shape concert

Canadian multimedia artist Nobuo Kubota created the large and distinctive poster for the opening week of Roy Thomson Hall.

Courtesy of Nobuo Kubota.

venues of the future, a future they were actively building not only in Toronto, but also in San Francisco, Baltimore, and Melbourne. Although Baltimore's Meyerhoff Hall was slightly smaller than the others, each of these venues exceeded capacity for 2,500 ticket holders, purely for economic reasons. In designing their interiors, Schultz believed that the listener would benefit most from the sounds coming from the front and then reflecting from the back of the hall. It was an assumption that led to bringing the auditorium's back wall forward, thereby widening the narrow rectangle embodied in many of the major European halls, and building in a more circular shape.

Both Schultz and Erickson had learned from the field of psychoacoustics the role our eyes play in reinforcing the evidence of our ears, and had given the cultivation of intimacy a high priority. The price of their achievement was to lessen the impact of reflections from side walls in bringing resonance and warmth to the sound. It wasn't until Roy Thomson Hall was being used for its intended purpose that it became obvious to ticket buyers that seats in the centre of the space provided a substantially different listening experience than those situated around its perimeter.

Working relationships between acousticians and architects are seldom easy. Witnesses report that the American acoustician Russell Johnson of Artec Consultants Inc. and the French architect Jean Nouvel clashed repeatedly before producing one of the most highly praised modern concert halls in Europe for the KKL Culture and Convention Centre in Lucerne, Switzerland. It's unsurprising, then, that there was some tension between Theodore Schultz and Arthur Erickson. For Schultz, the challenge of producing a series of new halls in unorthodox shapes necessarily involved a degree of experimentation. Keith Loffler recalls how the acoustician would make frequent changes to his plans, requiring Erickson to follow suit. This became a source of irritation, with Erickson exclaiming after one meeting, "I wish that guy would make up his mind!" Budget issues also came into play. According to Loffler, Bolt, Beranek and Newman had promised to bring in their contribution to New Massey Hall within the originally specified budget, which necessitated some cuts in the final execution. One of the casualties of cost-cutting was soundproof trap doors that were to seal the attic openings for the hanging acoustical rods off from the auditorium. This change allowed sound to escape up into the cavernous space above the concert hall.

Initially, at least, it appeared that Schultz had kept up his side of the bargain, despite the modifications to the original plan. One of the first accounts of sound in the completed hall came from Arnold Edinborough of the *Financial Post*, who had snuck in to witness acoustical tests in May of 1982. He described the Toronto Symphony Orchestra and the Toronto Mendelssohn Choir singing the "Hallelujah Chorus" from *Messiah*:

As those noble notes died away, Andrew Davis stepped onto the stage and conducted the whole thing again while [Elmer] Iseler roamed around the mezzanine and the ground floor. When Davis came to the end of that great piece, he turned to the mezzanine: "Well, Elmer?" "Fantastic," said Iseler, and the governors sitting dotted around the great space breathed a $40 million sigh of relief: the acoustics were basically okay.

While the architectural and acoustical teams had worked out a semblance of collaborative spirit, Erickson was a stickler for detail in anything that concerned his work — or that of his life and business partner, interior designer Francisco Kripacz, who had conceived the hall's interior finishes. Building committee member John Lawson, who would in 1989 succeed Edward Pickering as president of the board, recalls the entire building committee being summoned by the architect

The building has dramatic curving lobbies.

Photo by Shin Sugino.

to an emergency meeting at the construction site, only to discover that Erickson was upset because a small sample piece of carpeting for the concert hall's floors had arrived not matching the exact shade of grey he had specified. Grey was to be the hall's signature colour, its choice representing a way of integrating concrete surfaces with upholstery and carpeting into a visual continuum. Achieving the perfect shade was, for Erickson, not simply a creative whim.

The architect hoped that audiences would provide most of the colour to the building, not least of all in the spacious lobbies, where they were to be seen through the surrounding glass walls at night. As Erickson put it, the place would be "a spectacle of light, never looking empty but always animated, showing how a static building mass can be a lively visual asset to a city." The problem with this plan was that the high levels of lobby lighting necessary to make patrons visible to passersby generated a lot of heat. Erickson's daytime objective — to have the honeycombed glass exterior reflect the neighbouring city and the surrounding sky — proved more realistic, especially since the only way to make glass more energy efficient at the time was to coat it with a mirrored surface.

Even in its modified state and notwithstanding prominent *Globe and Mail* columnist Colin Vaughan complaining that the design scarcely mirrored the character of a red-brick city, Roy Thomson Hall was greeted as an iconic build- ing. Calling it a "semi surround hall where some seating wraps around the platform for visual and acoustic intimacy despite a large audience capacity," the British architectural historian Michael Forsythe featured it prominently in a comprehensive 1985 book, *Buildings for Music*. He drew special attention to the adjustability of its reverberation time, a feature unknown in concert halls of the past but obviously of use in a hall intended to serve various styles of music from different centuries. To make this adjustable acoustic possible, the performing arts extended a friendly hand to the visual arts, as the design of the colourful tubes flying from the ceiling was commissioned from Quebec tapestry artist Mariette Rousseau-Vermette. "Coloured white, cream, red and burgundy, they were conceived as a three-dimensional tapestry, which for cer- tain works would make the entire ceiling appear to open like the petals of a flower," wrote Forsythe.

In an interview for the house magazine, *BRAVO*, Erickson did not disguise his pride when he noted:

> There's never been a hall designed like it. The interior is going to
> be fantastic. We've avoided what I've hated in all halls forever —
> that they have a box and a plaster thing inside which has nothing
> to do with the structure or with anything. All the recent halls — in
> Minneapolis, San Francisco, Melbourne — have this meaningless

The stage as seen from inside the attic.

plaster gimmickry inside. The Roy Thomson Hall is absolutely pure. Everything is there for a purpose. It achieves a certain grace and the scale is fantastic.

Acknowledging the hall as a departure from his own past practice, Erickson went on to celebrate the building and the team that built it:

I've never done anything like it. The workmanship and concrete work are extraordinary. People have no idea how difficult it is working in curves…. People tend to focus on the architect. To accomplish something like that takes so many people. If you're a good architect, all you are is a kind of tuning fork, picking up the vibrations in the air and trying to bring them together.

The humility embodied in this statement paid tribute to a decade of collaborative enterprise, beginning with the board's proposal that Erickson, as chief design architect, work in tandem with the Toronto firm of Mathers and Haldenby, who were the architects of record at Massey Hall for a number of years. The *Globe and Mail*'s architecture critic, Lisa Rochon, captured the essence of Erickson's accomplishment when she wrote his obituary in May 2009: "Erickson was a master with concrete, a material he once described as 'the marble of our time.'"

Unfortunately, due to a number of strikes in the construction industry, the initial three years projected for the hall's completion turned into four. Even so, a jubilant Pickering greeted the results as a triumph:

> Hundreds of people have given their time, energy and talent to create this spectacular new landmark for Toronto. All our basic concepts seem to be coming true. We said we wanted an architecturally exciting hall. We've got that. We said we wanted a hall that would be comfortable for performers and patrons and we believe we have got that. Above all we wanted a hall with superlative sound, and the indications are we're getting that for our orchestra, organ, choir and soloists.
>
> Massey Hall served Toronto well for nearly 90 years. It was appropriate for its time. But now we've built a highly contemporary hall to take its place, in an era when what happens inside the hall can be heard and seen around the world. And we hope that it will be so good that it will occupy a significant place in the global scheme of things, not just as a purely Toronto facility.
>
> Now the real test will come when the concert-going public comes through its doors. They will tell us what they think.

CHAPTER 3

Gabriel Kney's King of Instruments

M OST PEOPLE IN the West associate the pipe organ with spiritual worship, but the mechanical assemblage of pipes, keyboards, and pedals that Mozart called the King of Instruments also has a long history in show business. As new public concert halls were built in the nineteenth century and the size of symphony orchestras grew, so did the role of the pipe organ. This is especially the case in the English-speaking world, which celebrated the marriage of organ and secular group singing in the form of choral societies that welcomed hundreds of singers at a time. There is hardly a town hall in England that doesn't boast a massive Victorian-era pipe organ that is still used in regular public concerts today.

A traditional organ is made up of dozens of sets of pipes, some metal, others constructed of wood. Each set is crafted to create defined sounds, many imitating specific wind and even string instruments in an orchestra. An organist can choose different combinations of pipes for any piece of music and change these combinations on the fly, resulting in rich, colourful, and sometimes very loud orchestra-like mixes.

Pipe organs can be as small as a "portatif" single-keyboard model less than one metre deep and two metres wide. These models are enclosed in a wooden case and placed on wheels, for use in playing baroque organ concertos, such as those by George Frideric Handel, or in continuo, which is the music that accompanies recitative in baroque and early classical opera and oratorio. But these miniaturized instruments are too puny for modern symphonic repertoire in large concert halls.

With the advent of electricity, inventors came up with motorized blower systems to replace the manual pumps that kept the air moving inside an organ's pipes. Until that time, the console's keyboards and pedal-board contained an intricate system of levers and rods directly connected to each pipe, manually opening and shutting off the air supply. The more pipes connected to each note, the harder it would be to press down each key, making the organist's job more difficult in passages requiring a lot of volume.

In the late nineteenth century, more adventurous organ builders began replacing these mechanical controls with pneumatic systems that harnessed the instrument's air pressure with a maze of small metal tubes. As electronic technology advanced, contacts, wires, and magnets took on the internal switching tasks — but some organists claimed that these power-operated advances were robbing them of the true "feel" of a mechanical action.

The fully electronic organ was born in the 1930s, with sound generated not by a vibrating column of air but electromagnetically, producing a completely different sort of tone, one most familiar to lovers of jazz in the wa-wa stylings of the Hammond organ. Electric organs finally allowed concerts requiring a pipe organ to be held in buildings that did not have a resident instrument. Recent great leaps forward in digital technology have created a booming industry in electronic organs that reproduce sounds sampled from the pipes of the world's largest and most famous acoustic instruments, further bolstering the arguments from people who believe that, for the vast majority of listeners, a digital reproduction is as good as the acoustic original. But while the pipes sitting inside the elaborately carved and gilded cases of many original sixteenth-century organs are still in regular use in Europe, the silicone chips and circuit boards feeding today's digital facsimiles may not be able to generate pleasant sounds five centuries from now.

Because of a pipe organ's tonal versatility, many large movie palaces and converted vaudeville theatres installed them to increase the range of possibilities for accompanying silent films. The most elaborate theatre organs were made by the Rudolph Wurlitzer Company in the United States, and would usually include an array of percussion sound effects, such as horses' hooves, gongs, and bells. One such Wurlitzer organ is housed in Toronto's Casa Loma, and is frequently used in concerts featuring old movie and theatre music.

In the concert hall, however, composers married the power of the pipe organ with the symphony orchestra. The resulting Symphony No. 3 (known as the Organ Symphony) by Camille Saint-Saëns (1835–1921), concertos by such composers as Josef Rheinberger (1839–1901) and Alexandre Guilmant (1837–1911), and large-scale symphonic works such as *The Planets* by Gustav Holst (1874–1934) and *Also sprach Zarathustra* by Richard Strauss (1864–1939) cemented the relationship. The 1938 Organ Concerto by Francis Poulenc (1899–1963) is the best-known piece in

Organ builder Gabriel
Kney, in the organ loft of
Roy Thomson Hall, 1982.

Photo by Nancy Westaway.

The organ's façade of soaring chrome pipes forms a dramatic focus for seats in the hall.

a massive surge of works for the combination of organ and orchestra written in the twentieth century.

Despite the growing popularity of symphonic music containing the organ, the Toronto Symphony Orchestra made do with borrowed instruments for many years. The builders of Massey Hall had not foreseen the need to install a pipe organ, but one was brought in and set up on a pedestal at the back of the stage early in the building's history, and then removed as part of the renovations undertaken in the 1930s. If a concert presenter didn't want to take over a church for the occasion, real pipe organs available for an evening's entertainment were available in the ballroom at the Royal York Hotel or the Eaton Auditorium. Because the popularity of the pipe organ declined after the Second World War, the Royal York Hotel sold its instrument to First Baptist Church in Jackson, Mississippi. When Eaton's moved its headquarters to the Eaton Centre in the mid-1970s, the auditorium was locked and the organ was sold to another Baptist church, in Dallas, Texas. At the time, the only remaining pipe organ in a concert auditorium in Toronto was a modest instrument at Walter Hall, on the University of Toronto campus, which seats only 490 people.

These disparate strands of history and trivia all became intertwined in the dreams for what was to become Toronto's premier concert organ at Roy Thomson Hall. Because everyone involved in the planning knew that this would be the permanent home of the Toronto Symphony Orchestra, there was a determined push to include a pipe organ capable of being used as a solo concert instrument as well as a symphonic partner.

A committee struck by the board of governors to consider the new pipe organ included Toronto Symphony Orchestra music director Andrew Davis, who had trained as an organist at King's College, Cambridge University. He was joined by two Canadian organists, Hugh McLean and George Brough. Fellow committee members included board representatives Keith MacMillan (son of long-time TSO music director Sir Ernest) and John Lawson. MacMillan charged McLean with the task of coming up with the specifications for an ideal concert instrument.

Lawson recalls how the estimate for McLean's dream organ came in at $750,000, but the original budget had been set at $500,000 — and even this lower amount seemed extravagant to many of the people who were involved in raising money to build the new hall. So McLean was asked to whittle down his wish list. "I had a hell of a time as it was convincing the building committee to include the cost of the organ in the campaign," recalls Lawson. But he persevered. Like many of the people on the board of governors at the time, Lawson had toured abroad with the Toronto Symphony Orchestra and had been a member of the Toronto Mendelssohn Choir, so had come to appreciate the musical and aesthetic value of having a great instrument alongside the orchestra and choir on stage.

Lawson and the organ committee had a key advocate in Andrew Davis. In a 1984 interview with Christopher Hume for *BRAVO*, the conductor admitted that he "sometimes had to fight" to make sure the organ project would come to fruition.

The logical place to turn for a concert-quality instrument was Casavant Frères in Saint-Hyacinthe, Quebec. Founded in 1879, the storied builder has to date installed nearly four thousand pipe organs around the world. Its most recent concert hall creations include instruments for Montreal's Maison symphonique, the new home of the Montreal Symphony Orchestra, and for the John F. Kennedy Center for the Performing Arts in Washington, D.C. But the sound and makeup

Released in 1984, Andrew Davis's album of solo organ pieces was recorded during two nights with page-turning assistance from Marquis Records' executive producer Deborah MacCallum.

Gabriel Kney's
Opus 95. Through
special arrangement,
the organ is used as
a teaching facility
for organ students of
the Faculty of Music,
University of Toronto.

of pipe organs is subject to changing tastes and fads, like the length of a skirt hem or the width of a jacket lapel. In the 1970s, most pipe organ builders were in the throes of a back-to-basics movement that eschewed electric action in favour of mechanical levers, and that promoted a sharper, more focused tonal palette influenced by the baroque-era organs of Saxony, in Germany. The person in charge of voicing Casavant organs in the day was an extreme proponent of this sound, which was and remains incompatible with modern symphonic music. "That cost Casavant the job right off the bat," says Lawson.

The job of building the organ was turned over to a small but accomplished workshop in London, Ontario, founded by Gabriel Kney, whose work was also informed by the so-called North German School, but who was more flexible in its execution. Born in Speyer am Rhein, Germany, in 1929, Kney grew up next to the city's eleventh-century cathedral, and learned his craft nearby. He eventually left for Canada, opening his own business in London, Ontario, in 1955. By the time Kney retired in 2006, Gabriel Kney Pipe Organ Builders had completed 129 organs for churches and halls in Canada and the United States.

Before making a commitment, the committee visited and tried a number of the maker's other instruments, and came away impressed. Of particular interest to the committee was Kney's ability to build two different consoles to control the pipes: one attached to the organ case using a purely mechanical action, and a second one powered by electricity, which could easily be moved to centre stage and connected to the pipework with an electric umbilical cord. At the time, the Sydney Opera House was the only concert hall with this sort of two-console organ. Since the Roy Thomson Hall instrument was ordered, two-console actions have become commonplace in large installations.

Another challenge facing everyone involved in the project was timing. As Lawson points out, the vast majority of pipe organs are designed and installed in conventional rectangular buildings, or are specified after a structure is complete. But the builders and planners of Roy Thomson Hall had to specify a certain size and type of instrument for a large, unconventional space that existed only in a series of sketches. Although an experienced organ designer, Kney had to go by the architects' and acousticians' estimates on reverberation times — educated guesses that did not always prove to be accurate in the days before computer-aided modelling became the norm.

Kney's original design for Opus 95 had 5,207 individual pipes arranged in seventy-one ranks and split into six groupings called tonal divisions, housed in a wide oak-stained case above the choir stalls at the front of the hall. But Arthur Erickson was not going to let anything stand out in his grey-on-grey colour palette; the architect was adamant that the audience and the cylindrical acoustic banners that hung from the original ceiling were all the visual distraction anyone needed in the enjoyment of music. To this end, Erickson proposed a tall, ten-metre-wide grey case dominated by silvery pipes and, for the tonal divisions that were to be under expression, acrylic shutters, a look and layout that has remained unchanged.

The construction estimate for this instrument came in at $650,000. It took ten craftspeople twenty thousand hours to make the casework, pipes, and mechanism in London. The loose parts were shipped to the construction zone at King and Simcoe Streets in two moving vans before the building's interior ceiling was finished. Using an elaborate system of ropes and pulleys fastened to the roof girders, Kney and his team lifted the organ's components into place and assembled everything on site. Because this was now a working instrument sitting in a real auditorium, Kney and his colleagues spent hundreds more hours adjusting the sound of each pipe to suit the new space.

Toronto Symphony Orchestra music director Andrew Davis ensured that Kney's Opus 95 would get pride of place at the gala opening concert on September 13, 1982, by programming Poulenc's Organ Concerto, with Hugh McLean as the soloist at the moveable console. Later that week, Davis acted as host of an organ concert titled "An Evening with the King of Instruments," with McLean, then-young Toronto organist Michael Bloss (who, three decades later, remains an occasional soloist with the Toronto Symphony Orchestra), University of Toronto organ professor John Tuttle, and Montrealer Mireille Lagacé.

Judy Stephenson, John Lawson, and guest organist Hugh McLean and his wife Anne, at the hall's gala opening, 1982.

Action Photographics.

During the opening season, the late American concert organist Carlo Curley declared his "love to a most fantastic hall and organ" in the Roy Thomson Hall guest book. He was so enamoured of the instrument's possibilities that the organist decided to record on the instrument. John Lawson recalls Curley also offering his services as a permanent resident curator, in exchange for being provided with living accommodations nearby — a suggestion Lawson says the board never took seriously. The Toronto Symphony Orchestra music director was the first to record his appreciation of the instrument in an album simply titled *Andrew Davis Plays the Organ at Roy Thomson Hall*. Produced by then-fledgling Canadian Marquis Classics, the album took nearly a year to produce, from conception to master tapes, in 1983. In an interview at the time, Davis admitted that he had a lot of practicing to do before the recording crew could set foot in the hall. "I've hardly played at all during the last ten years except at weddings of friends and relatives. I had to get my hands and feet in shape," he told journalist Christopher Hume. It took months for calendar dates to line up, and the album was finally recorded in October 1983 over a series of sessions that began at 11:00 p.m. and ended at 5:00 a.m., so as to not disturb Roy Thomson Hall's regular programming.

Davis climbed atop the organ bench as frequently as he could. At the end of the first season, the music director opened a Toronto Symphony Orchestra concert with an organ solo of J.S. Bach's popular Toccata and Fugue in D Minor — and ended it with Leopold Stokowski's orchestral arrangement of the same pieces. In 1986 he wanted a grand organ sound for the large choruses in the Toronto Symphony Orchestra/Toronto Mendelssohn Choir *Messiah* recording (the Sir Thomas Beecham arrangement), which was recorded at Centre In The Square in Kitchener-Waterloo; with EMI engineers in tow, he returned to Roy Thomson Hall following the sessions to dub the organ parts.

Davis has continued to champion the organ in subsequent years as the Toronto Symphony Orchestra's conductor laureate, including a recent set of two concerts featuring music by (and arrangements of) Johann Sebastian Bach in the fall of 2011. With John Tuttle collaborating, Ian Sadler, a well-known Ontario organist, recorded an album, *Duets & Solos for Organ*, on the instrument. And Diane Bish, the most prominent American concert organist of the last generation, has posted several YouTube videos of her solo work at the moveable stage console at Roy Thomson Hall.

The venue's programmers included many solo organ concerts in their initial seasons, and in 1989 Organ Explorations was launched, with local organists and students providing demonstrations with a history of the organ. Organ Explorations was kicked off with a Saturday open house on October 21, 1989, when the public was invited to "Perform Live at Roy Thomson Hall — fulfill your fantasy by playing the world famous organ." Janice Price, then director of marketing and communications, thought the event would create some fun media buzz and was delightfully surprised when a lineup of organ enthusiasts formed on the Saturday morning, extending down Simcoe Street and around the block. Years later she created the same event when she was president and CEO of the Kimmel Center in Philadelphia and looking for profile for their newly installed organ.

Despite the initial public interest in the organ, it was difficult to sell tickets to organ recitals, and eventually evening performances were replaced by Twilight Concerts, held right after business hours, showcasing the finest organists of Canada, the United States, and Europe. Meanwhile, the Roy Thomson Hall volunteers ran tours on weekdays that included an organ recital every Wednesday with Simon Dyke and others. In 1997, the hall's new director of marketing and communications, Heather Clark, herself an organist, recommended free noontime concerts featuring choir and organ. Long-time supporter the Edwards Charitable Foundation generously increased its annual support to subsidize the series. By

The organ case stands ten metres high and has 5,207 pipes.

Photo by Richard Beland.

2013, that series had introduced sixty-eight concerts by thirty different choral ensembles and twenty-eight organists. The series has been especially popular as a showcase for Toronto's many excellent children's choirs.

As was the case with the acoustics at Roy Thomson Hall, not everyone was happy with the sound of Gabriel Kney's creation. In their illustrated survey book *Organs of Toronto*, published a few months before the acoustical renovations at the building were completed, authors Alan T. Jackson and James Bailey argued that "it was obvious from the beginning that the organ could not cope with the large space and dry acoustic." But this did not stop many musicians from Canada and other parts of the world from presenting colourful recitals. Kney returned to his Opus 95 a couple of times after the hall opened to tweak the sound by adjusting air pressure and voicing in response to acoustical modifications made by Theodore Schultz. The organ builder was back once again in 2002 after the hall had been lined with Canadian maple to go over the whole instrument to make the best of the new acoustic, which meant removing each one of its 5,207 pipes to adjust its tone. Olivier Latry, the titular organist at the Notre Dame Cathedral in Paris, in 2005 wowed audiences with the full power of this reinvigorated organ with a rousing interpretation of the Poulenc Concerto performed with the TSO, followed by a solo appearance the next day that included a raucous improvisation on the theme from *Hockey Night in Canada*.

The King of Instruments is alive and well, and happily ensconced at Roy Thomson Hall.

CHAPTER 4

Launching Roy Thomson Hall

A DAY BEFORE the balloons flew and the champagne flowed, Roy Thomson Hall mounted what is known in the industry as a hard-hat concert, to which the men and women who had poured the concrete, welded the steel beams, hammered the nails, and fitted the glass were invited to enjoy the fruits of their labours. Those labours had been considerable.

Actual construction of the hall had begun in 1978 with the demolition of the 1913–14 Canadian Pacific Express building and sheds that had been used to house gold during the First World War. Amid the rubble, workers discovered the building's unopened safe, although it promptly disappeared before anyone could examine the contents. The whole project was overseen by Eastern Construction, a firm with experience extending from hospitals and government buildings to universities and shopping centres. In this case, Eastern was charged with erecting a 30,000-square-metre concert hall on a muddy hectare. In its promotional materials for the project, the firm took its motto from the poet Robert Browning: "Burrow awhile and build, broad on the roots of things."

Pouring a thousand tonnes of reinforced concrete into a great hole in the ground turned out to be a complicated process requiring steel trusses radiating from a cylindrical hub to support the roof. "It wasn't a usual process at all," admitted Art Karantjas, contracts manager for the project. "We had to put on the roof before we built the sides." Working with structural engineers Carruthers and Wallace, Eastern confronted the need to erect a building within a building, the inner structure being an auditorium isolated from noise and vibrations, the outer portion

Facing page: Photo by Action Photographics.

Keith Loffler at the North Court, upon completion of the new landscaping in 1992.

Courtesy of Keith Loffler.

housing lobbies, service facilities, and underground parking. The project was divided into multiple tracks to enable parts of the complex to be priced and construction begun before the whole design was complete. For more than four years the Eastern team reported regularly to the board's building committee, charged with keeping a tight rein on the costs and holding the total down to $44 million. Denis Ludlow of the project administration office characterized the results as "a bargain, considering the complexity of the building. We would have had to pay much more if they didn't put the shovel in when they did."

Basically a concrete, steel, and glass structure, Roy Thomson Hall consumed 19,000 cubic metres of concrete, or about half as much as can be found in the CN Tower. And as impressive as its quantity was the quality of the finishing work both inside and out. The auditorium's curved walls had to be carefully sandblasted for smoothness as well as aesthetic effect, to achieve uniform sound reflection. To refine the "downkickers," the three-dimensional curves near the top of the auditorium, Eastern used a Swiss surveying instrument usually employed in highway construction. With this instrument, even 360-degree angles could be measured by sending out infrared signals from the centre of the auditorium floor.

If the inner building presented special challenges, so did the outer building, which required the installation of a 3,700-square-metre glass canopy. Considerably simplified from its original design, it nevertheless had to be flown in piece by piece and fitted into place with the assistance of a special crane. Extra-large air conditioning ducts were chosen to ensure that heated or cooled air would flow silently into the public spaces (interestingly, these ducts were replaced with even larger-diameter units during the 2002 acoustical renovation). The walls hid several kilometres' worth of electrical and communications cabling to control the building's climate and stage and house lighting, as well as the live-broadcast needs of television and radio. And 1,800 square metres of mirrors added glamour to the lobbies. As construction manager William Elliott remarked, "Everything was done slowly and carefully. There are few standard things in the whole building."

Roy Thomson Hall's footprint includes what is called the North Court, a sunken concrete-lined garden with a sixty-five-metre-long, twenty-five-centimetre-deep reflecting pool. The courtyard runs along the property's King Street side, five metres below the street level, sitting above the parking garage. As an architect known for his response to the natural environment, Arthur Erickson had collaborated with EVM Landscape Architects Emile G. van der Meulen and J. Brian McCluskey to soften his building's concrete and glass profile while simultaneously bringing light into the administrative offices on its lower floor. At the outdoor reception held in the North Court following the hall's opening, Lois Wilson, vice-chair of the Dunnington Grubb Foundation responsible for the sunken garden's grant donation, reportedly asked Erickson where the laurels were. When she explained that she wanted to make a crown for him, he reportedly replied with atypical modesty for an architect, "It would not become me."

At the time of Roy Thomson Hall's tenth anniversary, the Garden Club of Toronto was invited to redesign the garden. Landscape designer Dorothea Lovat Dickson, a member of the club, donated her services to plan the Muskoka-inspired layout that is still visible today. Few passersby on the PATH concourse, which runs at water level, or along King Street realize that the boulders are not real rocks, but imitations carefully wrought from composite materials. A pleasant spot for receptions and warm-weather takeout lunches, the North Court's treed islands have even played intermittent host to families of ducks, who properly regard it as a sanctuary within the concrete canyon-scape of downtown Toronto.

The Garden Club of Toronto celebrates the redesign of the North Court, 1992.

Make way for the ducklings, an annual spring event.

Ken Faught / GetStock.com.

Although it has since been turned into a surface parking lot, a grassy South Court originally graced the Wellington Street side of the property, offering space for the possible future addition of a recital hall and enabling nearby office workers to take a noon-hour respite beneath the shade of its honey locust trees.

The careful, deliberate planning that had gone into realizing the dream of a New Massey Hall played itself out on a different scale in the preparations for the opening celebrations of Roy Thomson Hall. John Arena of Winston's, one of Toronto's finest restaurants in the day, had been put in charge of properly feeding and refreshing a VIP opening-night guest list over the course of the evening. To ensure that everything would go according to plan, he even organized a number of trial runs so that he could ensure that food and drink prepared at three different locations would arrive in precise synchronization for the pre-concert, intermission, and post-concert festivities.

For the pre-concert dinner for two thousand, he prepared a feast that included smoked sturgeon, oysters, pâté de foie gras, truffles, and pyramids of shrimp and lobster. More lobster medallions were served to the audience during intermission (a visiting scribe from Northern California confessed that he had never before seen so much lobster) and, before saying good night, patrons were invited to top up their plates with gâteau St. Honoré and chocolate truffles. More than two hundred cooks, servers, and assistants prepared and served the food, which was washed down with nearly two thousand bottles of wine and champagne, fifty-six litres of cognac, and a thousand mugs of Irish coffee. By evening's end, the sixteen ice sculptures that had shared space with an array of stuffed wild birds decorating the service tables had begun to melt their way into history.

The high spirits were palpable that warm night of September 12, 1982. Governor General Edward Schreyer and Premier William Davis were present, as was the hall's feted architect, who turned up with Pamela Buckley, wife of the acid-tongued American columnist William F. Buckley Jr., on his arm. "I love it," enthused Mayor Art Eggleton. "There's not a bad word to be said about this hall. We should be very proud."

Nor was the hall's principal benefactor in a mood to disagree with him. "The verdict was prejudged and it was prejudged correctly," volunteered Ken Thomson. "There's not a discordant note in the entire building."

Top: Ken Thomson arrives on opening night.

Courtesy of *The Globe and Mail*.

Bottom left: Douglas McGibbon and Pauline McGibbon, Lieutenant Governor of Ontario, on opening night.

Bottom right: Marilyn and Ken Thomson on opening night.

Bottom photos by Action Photographics.

The hall as seen from the west.

Douglas Aitken, president and CEO of Marathon Realty, and John Lawson, chair of the Board of Governors, 1988–93, and president, 1988–92. The plaque that they are standing in front of reads, in part, "The land on which Roy Thomson Hall sits was donated by Marathon Realty Company Limited, a subsidiary of Canadian Pacific Limited."

Photo by Brian Pickell, 1992.

The $44-million building had witnessed its official opening earlier in the day, at its Simcoe Street main entrance, with the cutting of a silver-grey ribbon bearing the victory motif from Beethoven's Fifth Symphony, and the launching of a thousand silver-coloured, helium-filled balloons in the presence of dignitaries wearing "We Made It" badges. For a select group of VIPs that day, the evening didn't end until they visited a reception hosted by Erickson at his Rosedale coach house — an event so well attended that Toronto police were called in to manage traffic in the usually quiet neighbourhood.

The events of September 12 were nearly upstaged by a

private concert held two weeks earlier, when the Canadian Bar Association kicked off a week-long conference with a rare recital by the great Canadian tenor Jon Vickers in the hall. No members of the media or the general public were admitted to the event, since Theodore Schultz had yet to complete his final acoustical adjustments and wanted to avoid the slightest possibility of the sorts of negative reviews that had greeted the hasty opening of his sister hall a year earlier in San Francisco. Fresh from knee surgery, Vickers walked onstage with the support of a cane, declaring that this was an event he could not miss.

When the opening night reviews did appear, they turned out to be more favourable than those that saluted San Francisco's Louise M. Davies Symphony Hall. "Uncork the bubbly. Toronto has come up with a winner," announced the *Toronto Star*'s critic William Littler. In the *Globe and Mail*, critic John Kraglund characterized the opening concert as "a resounding success." American reviewers seemed no less welcoming, with Byron Belt of the Newhouse newspaper chain declaring that "the most dazzling of several new concert halls that have opened recently on this continent is clearly Roy Thomson Hall." Richard Pontzious of the *San Francisco Examiner* echoed him: "It's a wonderful hall, simple yet consistently elegant — a tribute to what can be done with massive blocks of unpainted concrete, matching carpeting and indirect lighting. But there's more. Not only does it look fashionably austere … but wonder of wonders, it has the kind of acoustics that Bay Area concertgoers dream about." As if to testify that he hadn't quite lost his critical faculties, Pontzious then added, "If there's a negative aspect to the hall it's to be found outside. The building looks like a hat taken off a Southeast Asian farmer and set on the ground." His counterpart on the *San Francisco Chronicle*, Robert Commanday, actually likened it to an "inverted cupcake." Everyone present, along with thousands of people across the country who followed the live broadcasts by CBC Radio and Television, witnessed a program deliberately designed to show off the new venue's versatility.

Usher captains in 1988, Sharon Kee, Janet Connolly, and house manager Chris Perry supervised the sixty-member ushering staff.

Photo by Doug Tigani.

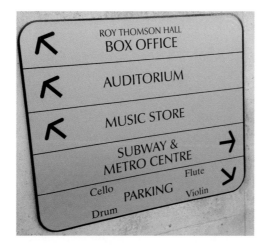

Even the parking garage
has orchestral sections.

Photo by Peter O'Brien.

Opening the evening was a fan-fare chosen from fifty-two entries submitted in a competition. Toronto Symphony Orchestra music director Andrew Davis, who personally chose the winner from entries that had been presented anonymously, picked a piece written by associate principal clarinetist and composer Raymond Luedeke for trumpets, full orches-tra, and organ. Roy Thomson Hall's two principal tenants had a chance to show off together in a performance of William Walton's oratorio *Belshazzar's Feast*, featuring among its starry soloists baritone Victor Braun, father of Canadian baritone Russell Braun. Canada's most brilliant organist of the day, Hugh McLean, added a blast of sound from the gleaming pipework of Gabriel Kney's Opus 95 in the Organ Concerto by Poulenc. The Toronto Mendelssohn Choir, under artistic director Elmer Iseler, sang unaccompanied Canadian pieces by R. Murray Schafer and former Toronto Symphony Orchestra music director Sir Ernest MacMillan.

Robert Commanday found the sound in *Belshazzar's Feast* "at times over-whelming," and Robert Finn of the *Cleveland Plain Dealer*, although he regarded the sound as "extremely clear" and with "excellent presence," complained of a lack of string tone from the orchestra. Robert Croan of the *Pittsburgh Post-Gazette*, with a few similar reservations, took solace in the thought that the hall's "acoustics may be adjusted after the opening."

Six more days of successive concerts followed the opening, with Canada's Snowbird, Anne Murray, taking centre stage the next night and a semi-staged presentation by the Canadian Opera Company of Richard Strauss's *Capriccio* (including a pas de deux by famed National Ballet of Canada dancers Karen Kain and Frank Augustyn), a celebration of the Gabriel Kney organ, a children's gala (featuring the Canadian Children's Opera Chorus), a matinee solo recital by the great soprano Lois Marshall, an evening with Gordon Lightfoot, and a massed choir celebration completing the week.

The week did not proceed without glitches, such as a lobby fire alarm that inter-rupted Anne Murray's concert. But a spirit of celebration held sway, and included a South German wine-pipe ceremony at the organ concert. Gabriel Kney appeared on stage in formal evening dress, complete with white gloves, to dispense champagne to everyone on stage with the help of an organ-pipe-shaped pipette. Once emptied, the pipette was handed over as a present to Edward Pickering, whose family still keeps the vessel as a treasured artifact.

CHAPTER 5

A Home for the Toronto Symphony Orchestra

W HEN CANADIANS FIRST saw the opening-night interior of Roy Thomson Hall on CBC Television, arrayed on stage for the celebration were the nearly one hundred members of the Toronto Symphony Orchestra and their affable music director, Andrew Davis, turned out in white tie and tails. This was a housewarming that had been nearly two decades in the making, offered up with smiles and passion.

Unseen and unheard that night was the tug of a basic equation that, thirty years later, continues to play a pivotal role in the ties between the Toronto Symphony Orchestra and its home — an equation that has, through subtle shifts in power dynamics and economic imperatives, shaped every facet of that relationship. Every symphony orchestra needs a concert hall, but not every concert hall has, or can handle, a symphony orchestra.

How this equation has worked itself out has its roots back at Massey Hall. The Grand Old Lady of Shuter Street was in many ways an ideal home for symphonic concerts. As soon as the Toronto Symphony Orchestra had taken its current form in the early 1920s, the two organizations were able to thrive and feed on each other's good fortunes.

"It is doubtful that the orchestra's long-term success would have been as assured if it had not been blessed with the only 'pure' concert hall in Canada," wrote the *Globe and Mail*'s music critic John Kraglund in 1982. "And it must be assumed that Massey Hall would not necessarily have developed as Toronto's musical centre if the Toronto Symphony had not been located there."

Andrew Davis, the TSO's music director from 1975 to 1988.

But Massey Hall had not been conceived with the needs of a resident orchestra in mind, so from the Toronto Symphony Orchestra's point of view there were perennial inconveniences involving the lack of backstage space for anything more than hanging up a winter coat.

In *Begins with the Oboe*, a history of the Toronto Symphony Orchestra, Richard Warren described how music scores in the small Massey Hall library were stacked so high that a ladder was often needed to pick them off the shelves. "The green room was not a green room but an area adorned by portraits," Warren wrote. There was no lounge for the musicians. But, not wanting to completely disregard the need for a bit of backstage distraction, there was a ping pong table and, for the more sedate artist, a card table.

As time went on and the world modernized, audiences began to grumble about the stairs, cramped lobby areas, insufficient washroom accommodations, and significant number of seats with imperfect sightlines.

For more than a decade in the post–Second World War boom years, there had been quiet talk among patrons about how nice it would be if the Toronto Symphony Orchestra and its building mate, the Toronto Mendelssohn Choir, could get a new, purpose-built home. Without a determined push from the orchestra, a new concert hall large enough to accommodate it would not come to be.

The person who turned these dreams and wish lists into an action plan was Edward Pickering. An executive with the long-defunct Simpson's department store chain (which was absorbed by Sears), Pickering joined the board of the Toronto Symphony Orchestra in 1961, becoming president in 1964. In reminiscences collected from Pickering's years with the orchestra, musicians described how this active board president took the time to learn their children's names, would remember birthdays and, most importantly, pushed hard to increase the organization's season from thirty weeks to forty-two. Ruth Budd, one of the symphony's double bass players at the time, recalled how Pickering "tried very much to dissolve that line between board and players."

By the time he completed his three-year tenure as board president, Pickering had ensured a raise in the musicians' base pay from $130 to $180 a week. The Toronto Symphony Orchestra Foundation had been established to secure the organization's long-term financial health. Pickering had also determined that the only way for the Toronto Symphony Orchestra to grow artistically as well as in audience development was to build itself a new home.

The match that lit Pickering's fire was Seiji Ozawa, a fiery Japanese conductor who was only thirty when he conducted his first TSO concert as music director in 1965. When Czech conductor Karel Ancerl took over after Ozawa left for the San Francisco Symphony four years later, the Toronto Symphony Orchestra signed a recording contract with what was then known as CBS Records and inaugurated the first of a decade's worth of wildly popular summer seasons at Ontario Place, adding thousands of ticket buyers to its mailing list. A modern concert hall with balanced acoustics, great seats, easy accessibility, and enough washroom facilities for all became even more pressing.

At this point, the operations of Massey Hall and the Toronto Symphony Orchestra were inextricably bound. The orchestra had priority use of the hall's space, and the season's concert calendar was built around its principal tenant. Several members of the Massey Hall Board of Governors also belonged to the board of the Toronto Symphony Orchestra. Pickering became one of those people in 1972, the year he retired from what was then Simpsons-Sears. For the next five years, he served on both boards, and used that opportunity to push plans for New Massey Hall. "He was totally dedicated to whatever he was doing. Without him, I don't think Roy Thomson Hall ever would have been built," says John Lawson, who succeeded Pickering as president of the Corporation of Massey Hall and Roy Thomson Hall in 1988. Thanks to the Toronto Symphony Orchestra's input into

Günther Herbig, the TSO's music director from 1988 to 1994, and a young fan, Joshua Israelievitch.

Photo by Cylla von Tiedemann. Courtesy of City of Toronto Archives.

what extras needed to come with New Massey Hall, the new building included a large musicians' lounge, complete with waist-level shelving for instruments, ample locker space, change rooms with showers, and easy access to the stage. The loading zone on the Wellington Street side of the building was even placed on a level plane with the stage to make crews' jobs easier and to help safeguard valuable instruments and stage equipment.

Loie Fallis, director of artistic planning for the Toronto Symphony Orchestra, recalls how musicians struck a "large instrument committee" that worked with the planners and architects on how high and wide doorways and hallways needed to be in order to allow double basses and timpani to pass through without harm. "Judy Loman was asked how much space she would need for her harp," Fallis remembers. Also, the great American violinist Itzhak Perlman was consulted about backstage and stage access for people with physical challenges, something new to planners' lists of design considerations at the time. Among the rooms added to make the building more versatile, the new concert venue was to get a separate rehearsal hall large enough to seat the full orchestra and a soloist, or the full contingent of the Toronto Mendelssohn Choir. The plan was to move all rehearsals into this space so that programmers would be able to rent out the main auditorium for concerts and other events on nights when the Toronto Symphony Orchestra was not performing.

The new hall's acoustics were intended to provide each musician on stage with instant feedback, so no one would have to rely on guesswork. The auditorium would

Itzhak Perlman speaks with students from the Toronto Symphony Youth Orchestra backstage at Roy Thomson Hall, 1989.

Photo by Brian Pickell. Courtesy of City of Toronto Archives.

have its own organ to ensure that the Toronto Symphony Orchestra and Toronto Mendelssohn Choir could present the widest possible range of repertoire. It is no coincidence that music director Andrew Davis, who arrived in 1975 and became instantly popular with both the musicians and patrons, had trained as an

(Left to right) Robert R. Cranston, chair of the Board of Governors, 1993–95; Charles Cutts; and former Unitel vice-chairman George Harvey proudly present Unitel's sponsorship of the large external electronic sign, 1995.

organist in his native England. And, to satisfy the TSO's financial planners and marketers, the new hall would have at least as many "subscribable" seats as Massey Hall — all unhindered by uncomfortable viewing angles, supporting columns, or limited legroom, as had been the case in the old building.

Whether the need to get as close as possible to three thousand seats for symphony patrons helped contribute to Roy Thomson Hall's acoustical problems remains a point of debate. Many music lovers, musicians, and acousticians maintain that the traditional shoebox-shaped nineteenth-century concert hall, containing no more than two thousand seats, is the ideal for sound as well as intimacy.

The new space, on the other hand, promised no loss in ticket revenue for its masters, an adjustable acoustic for its users, and a round shape to bring all patrons into closer proximity with performers. "It would be very difficult to get a bad seat in Roy Thomson Hall," wrote the *Globe and Mail*'s Gary Michael Dault at the time of its opening. "The hall's sight-lines have been impeccably planned."

Beyond debate, however, were the behind-the-scenes difficulties that severely and repeatedly strained relations between the Toronto Symphony Orchestra and Roy Thomson Hall during the first two decades of the building's history.

On the surface, the transition from Victorian heap to twentieth-century concrete-glass-and-steel architectural monument was understood and portrayed as a step from past glories into a world of new possibilities. In that spirit, the orchestra's last season at Massey Hall, in 1981–82, was all about history and commemorations, featuring a parade of favourite guest conductors, culminating with a gala closing concert on June 4, 1982. The program included music from the Toronto Symphony Orchestra's first Massey Hall concert, on April 23, 1923, as well as a new composition, *A Farewell Tribute to the Grand Old Lady of Shuter Street*, by TSO trumpeter Johnny Cowell.

Symphony managers had encouraged audience members to wear clothing inspired by the 1920s for the event. The Toronto Transit Commission commandeered streetcars to take people straight from Shuter and Victoria Streets to Roy Thomson Hall after the concert. "There was a big red carpet laid across

Before the 2002 acoustical renovation, the ceiling of the hall included movable discs and textile-covered tubes, used for acoustical adjustments.

Photo by Action Photographics.

the stage," Fallis recalled. "People were invited to walk across the stage and have a glass of champagne." This was followed by a big supper for both patrons and members of the orchestra, hosted by theatre owner Ed Mirvish at Ed's Warehouse, a large restaurant he operated across the street, where the Princess of Wales Theatre now stands.

There were smiles and congratulations all around at every public event associated with the imminent opening of the new facility. Nearly everyone present was struck by how visually arresting and glamorous the new concert space looked, recalls former CBC Radio host Eric Friesen. The initial reviews on the acoustics may also have been favourable, but there were many frowns to be seen beneath the stairs in the new building's administrative office space, which is shared by both Roy Thomson Hall and Toronto Symphony Orchestra staff. In his unpublished memoir, Pickering wrote about conflicts over money and territory that had sprouted in the dealings between the two organizations as they made the transition to a new home:

> As the opening drew near, serious problems arose between the Boards of the Toronto Symphony and Roy Thomson Hall, due mainly to differing interpretations of the purpose of the new Hall and the role of the two organizations. In Massey Hall, the Symphony had become accustomed to the freedom of the place, having virtually the run of it to suit their needs. With the exception of the Toronto Mendelssohn Choir there were no other major users, and we allowed the Orchestra the widest latitude in day-to-day operations, especially in the years when all our energies were concentrated on the funding and construction of the new Hall. Some Symphony Board members and staff took for granted these conditions would continue when they moved into the new Hall. Because the Hall was

Mstislav Rostropovich and Seiji Ozawa, the TSO's music director from 1965 to 1969, at the Great Gathering, 1987.

Courtesy of the TSO.

being built as a facility to serve the specific needs of the Symphony, some of their directors assumed that they would operate it. A senior member of their board did indeed say to me that the job of our Board of Governors was simply to build the Hall and then turn it over as the home of the Symphony to run as they saw fit.

The first big dispute was over money. In its final season at Massey Hall, the Toronto Symphony Orchestra paid $328,237 in rent to its landlord, while its first year in the new building would end up costing it $997,503 — more than triple. It was no surprise that the orchestra and managing director Walter Homburger were upset at the huge increase in their organization's fixed expenses. Negotiations on the new rent were so difficult that, as Pickering's successor Lawson remembers, in order to get the lease agreement signed, the board of governors had to threaten to lock out the Toronto Symphony Orchestra two days before its moving trucks were set to arrive at the new building.

Pickering maintained that, given all of the extra space the orchestra was about to occupy, as well as the associated costs of maintaining it, a higher rent was entirely justified. A large portion of the construction costs of the new hall had come from three levels of government on the promise that the organization would not ask for any operating grants in the future, and Pickering was not about to break his word. The only way to ensure this was to make sure the building's managers and trustees were able to maximize revenue as a combination of landlord and music presenter.

The TSO celebrated its ninetieth season with special programming, including a performance of J.S. Bach's Concerto for Two Violins featuring Peter Oundjian (right) and his former teacher, Itzhak Perlman, 2012.

Photo by Dale Wilcox.

"Other contentious issues followed, among them the Symphony's claim to exclusive control of the scheduling of the auditorium for rehearsals and concerts; its refusal to accept the Hall's management of catering and control of the sale of alcoholic beverages; opposition to the Hall presenting the great orchestras of the world and soliciting sponsorships from business corporations," wrote Pickering in his personal notes.

In the process of addressing these problems, the old practice of cross-membership of board members between the two organizations collapsed. The catalyst was Homburger's other enterprise, a concert series he ran through the International Artists Concert Agency he had started in 1947 and had sold to the Toronto Symphony Orchestra shortly before it moved to Roy Thomson Hall.

As a not-for-profit organization paying rent to a not-for-profit landlord, the Toronto Symphony Orchestra had been assured that it was getting a preferential rate — a break that the board of the new hall was unwilling to extend to the for-profit concert business taken over from Homburger. The orchestra had also demanded preferential treatment in booking performers under the other concert series. This created a conflict with Roy Thomson Hall, which was also in the business of booking its own concerts in order to ensure that it would not incur a financial loss in its yearly operations.

Pickering admitted in his memoirs to having been blindsided by the storm that erupted in the two organizations' boardrooms:

There were three Past Presidents of the Toronto Symphony on our Board, Frank McEachren, Jim Westaway and myself, and two Past Presidents of the Women's Committee, Mary Ortved and Judy Simmonds, leading us mistakenly to assume that the Symphony would have no concern about their needs being understood and met.

In addition there were five members who sat on both Boards, including Frank McEachren, Marvin Gelber, and Ed Bovey, a senior Symphony Vice President. With these interlocking arrangements in place I for one and others assumed that communication was taking place on a regular basis. Unfortunately, this was not happening but we did not realize we had a communications problem until controversy had muddied the waters.

For reasons which he never made clear, Alan Marchment, President of the Toronto Symphony, took the position that, in view of the differences which had arisen, no one should sit on both Boards and asked the directors concerned to resign from one or the other. All five promptly resigned from the Symphony Board, including Mrs. Ortved and Mrs. Simmonds who were deeply offended by Alan's insistence in spite of their long years of service to the Symphony.

It took four years before some of these issues were resolved to everyone's satisfaction, thanks to a task force that had been set up with the cooperation of both organizations' boards. As Pickering, who was still president of the board at Roy Thomson Hall at that time, wrote in his memoir, the task force came up with an accord, "which in essence recognized our Board's right to manage the Hall and Symphony's right to be consulted and informed on matters of concern to them. In achieving this, they demonstrated that most problems can be resolved by men of good sense and good will reasoning together."

Ross Kennedy, a labour lawyer and long-time Toronto Symphony Orchestra and Roy Thomson Hall board member, mused many years later that the separation of the boards had ultimately been the right thing to do. "Symphonies shouldn't manage real estate. And halls shouldn't manage symphonies. Otherwise the orchestra ends up with a core group of only 70 players and no world-class conductor."

Among the long list of contentious topics during the hall's first two decades was the rehearsal hall, which Andrew Davis shunned in favour of holding rehearsals on stage. This struck one or two possible rental or concert dates from the Roy Thomson Hall rental calendar during every week of the TSO season. "We went in there very early on. I'm sure it was Richard Strauss *Ein Heldenleben*, I know it had to be something big, and it was just too loud," remembers Loie Fallis. "It was really uncomfortable, it was hurting people's ears. So then we used it for rehearsing Mozart and smaller things. It turned out to be an excellent rehearsal room for the Toronto Mendelssohn Choir."

Hoping to find a compromise that addressed the needs of all three organizations, the rehearsal hall was partially repurposed during the planning process for the 2002 acoustical renovations. By lowering the ceiling on the large room, the new upper space became a donors' lounge, which opened in 2004, conveniently located a few metres from the main entrance on Simcoe Street.

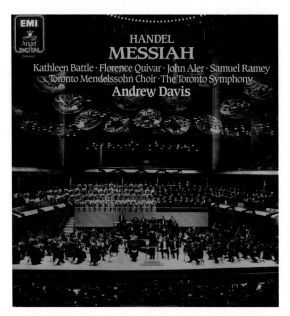

Despite Handel's *Messiah* being recorded at the Centre In The Square in Kitchener, Ontario, EMI/Angel requested that the interior of Roy Thomson Hall be the LP cover photograph.

Courtesy of EMI Classics.

Another constant irritant was the quality of sound inside Roy Thomson Hall. Despite the adjustable acrylic discs and hundreds of colourful, retractable circular banners that hung from the auditorium's ceiling, musicians and critics grew increasingly disenchanted with the building's dry sound with each passing year. The matter came to a head during the 1985–86 season, when the producers at record label EMI/Angel threatened to pull back from a promised recording of Gustav Holst's *The Planets* at the hall because "it was not up to their standards," wrote Richard Warren. The Toronto Symphony Orchestra ended up making this album as well as the next one — the still much-loved recording of Handel's *Messiah*, with Davis, soprano Kathleen Battle, mezzo-soprano Florence Quivar, tenor John Aler, and bass Samuel Ramey and the Toronto Mendelssohn Choir — at the more resonant main auditorium at Kitchener-Waterloo's Centre In The Square. In response, Pickering ordered the first of several reviews of the building's acoustics.

In the meantime, the Toronto Symphony Orchestra went through a period of prolonged internal turmoil that coincided with multiple changes in its leadership. Walter Homburger, who had been managing director of the orchestra since 1962, decided to retire at the end of the 1986–87 season, a prelude to Andrew Davis's final season as music director in 1987–88.

Most Torontonians remember the TSO musicians strike in the fall of 1999 and the near-bankruptcy in the fall of 2001, an event that changed its management structure, reduced the size of the all-volunteer board, and extracted big breaks in salaries from musicians as well as staff — and reductions in rent payable to Roy Thomson

Hall. Rather than being a surprise, that crisis had been foreshadowed nearly a decade earlier when, at the end of contract negotiations in 1992, the musicians rejected a 15 percent pay cut to help reduce the orchestra's mounting deficits. The following day, Toronto Symphony Orchestra management announced that it was looking into a voluntary filing for bankruptcy to force the issue. The musicians capitulated and gave in to the pay cut. The Ontario Place concerts were gone because programmers there decided they wanted more pop-oriented music. All touring was cancelled, and the organization hunkered down at Roy Thomson Hall in order to rebuild its fortunes.

But rather than strengthening itself, the orchestra's administrative side weakened further under a succession of permanent and temporary managing directors. In the fall of 1999, all of the musicians walked out on strike for nearly three months. Music director Jukka-Pekka Saraste felt compelled to go to Toronto mayor Mel Lastman to appeal for help in negotiating a solution. He succeeded in getting the players a pay raise — one they had to surrender again when the Toronto Symphony Orchestra ran out of cash in the fall of 2001.

The emergency funding that a restructured orchestra would receive came with strings attached. Former Ontario premier Bob Rae, an accomplished amateur pianist and supporter of the arts, agreed to be the public face of the process. In a 2002 speech to the Empire Club of Canada and the Canadian Club of Toronto, Rae said that it "is impossible to imagine a great city that does not have great musicians." There were deep changes involved, including slashing the size of the symphony board, obtaining compensation concessions from staff and musicians, and negotiating a substantial reduction in rent from its landlord.

Former PricewaterhouseCoopers partner Lambert Huizingh was appointed chief restructuring officer by symphony board chair Robert Weiss on September 28, 2001. Huizingh led a restructuring committee that included Rae in an advisory capacity, six board members, three musicians, and three representatives from the community. At the last minute, the Toronto Symphony Orchestra Foundation was given permission to transfer an initial $1.5 million in emergency funds to the organization, the first installment in a $5-million cash infusion that allowed the symphony to continue its 2001–02 season with minimal disruption.

Despite the fact that the symphony's crisis coincided with the launch of the acoustical renovations to the hall, the project was never in jeopardy. Current Corporation of Massey Hall and Roy Thomson Hall president and CEO Charles Cutts, who had taken over the administration of the venue in 1992, explains that the work was originally planned to begin in 2000, but a tight work schedule and the spectre of possible labour disruptions in the construction industry had already caused a two-year delay. Architects, engineers, and acousticians had been paid for their preparatory work, and pre-construction work to reinforce the building's ceiling had been completed. The Roy Thomson Hall board met on September 25,

2001, four days after Weiss had told musicians and staff that there was not enough money in the bank to cover the payroll that week. Cutts recalls how a number of different opinions regarding the project were expressed at the meeting, but positive voices prevailed. Board member Yoshio Nakatani, then president of Toyota Canada, rose to say, "Just like Lexus, which is the relentless pursuit of perfection, Roy Thomson Hall must go ahead with this project. It must be done."

"We have been the biggest sponsors of this orchestra for all these years," says Cutts, referring to the renovations paid for by the hall, as well as a series of reductions in the rent paid by the Toronto Symphony Orchestra over its three decades at its new home. During Cutts's first fiscal year, in 1991–92, the venue received $1,185,000 in rent from the orchestra. By 2011–12, the figure was down to $786,238.

The silver lining in this story is that the Toronto Symphony Orchestra's financial crisis, along with a brief move back to Massey Hall during the 2002 acoustical renovations to Roy Thomson Hall, appear in retrospect to have marked a significant turning point in the relationship between orchestra and landlord. The third decade has been the best one yet for working together cooperatively, with a revived orchestra as the main tenant in a rejuvenated building. The two organizations have also worked together to present classical soloists in Toronto — inviting guest artists to perform under the Roy Thomson Hall banner one season, then return as Toronto Symphony Orchestra guests the next.

"In recent years, we've been much better about being strategic about artists' futures here. Putting together long-term plans so that artists can come back every year, if they want to, in a different context," says Roy Thomson Hall's director of programming Jesse Kumagai. Adds Fallis: "It's about building an audience, a following." They cite week-long residencies by the Silk Road Ensemble, with Yo-Yo Ma, and pianist Lang Lang as notable examples of what both organizations can achieve when working together. To make sure both presenters know what is being planned, Cutts and Toronto Symphony Orchestra CEO Andrew Shaw have lunch together once a month, and the staff from the adjoining offices are encouraged to meet on a regular basis.

Even the two big Steinway concert grand pianos found in the auditorium are the products of cooperation. The Toronto Symphony Orchestra owns the New York–made piano, while Roy Thomson Hall owns the Hamburg-made one (recognizable by its glossy black finish) — yet the instruments, each costing more than $100,000 to replace, are made available to any artist performing in the hall, regardless of whether the concert is being presented by one organization or the other.

Thanks to some creative thinking on the part of both organizations, the building itself has served Toronto music fans in new ways, including as a setting for lobby concerts before and after Toronto Symphony Orchestra mainstage concerts. Recently the Young Leadership Council of the Toronto Symphony Orchestra has organized sold-out pre-concert tailgate parties for young professionals in what is probably the least inviting area of the property, the surface parking lot at the corner of Simcoe and Wellington Streets. Symphony management has even introduced a handful of casual concerts at which patrons can bring their drinks into the auditorium. Under current music director Peter Oundjian, Roy Thomson Hall has done double-duty as a recording studio, as the orchestra has released a string of live-concert recordings under its own TSOLive label.

Toronto Symphony Orchestra, Peter Oundjian, music director, 2012.

Photo by John Loper.

The Toronto Symphony Orchestra has also, over the years, adapted its schedule to help Roy Thomson Hall diversify its programming and offer events outside the classical music realm, including welcoming the Toronto International Film Festival and speakers' series such as Unique Lives & Experiences. It's a flexible, creative way of making the most out of the calendar that, according to Cutts, has helped the venue enjoy one of the highest usage rates of any concert hall in North America, averaging 310 performances and event bookings per year.

It's a spirit of creativity and sharing that bodes well for the next three decades.

A full stage: the Toronto Symphony Orchestra, Toronto Mendelssohn Choir, and Toronto Children's Chorus.

Photo by Paul J. Hoeffler.

CHAPTER 6

Singing the Praises of Choral Music

W HEN MOST TORONTONIANS think of classical concerts and Roy Thomson Hall, they associate them with the Toronto Symphony Orchestra, but choral music can also claim a strong bond with the place, thanks to the Toronto Mendelssohn Choir. This 150-person chorale, with a core group of professional singers, has been a fixture in the city for nearly three decades more than the Toronto Symphony — it was founded in 1894, the same year in which Massey Hall opened its doors. It was a tenured resident of the Grand Old Lady of Shuter Street long before a permanent orchestra arrived on the scene. Many members of the board of governors of the Corporation of Massey Hall and Roy Thomson Hall have sung with the Toronto Mendelssohn Choir, including former board chairs John Lawson, Suzanne Bradshaw, and Robert Cranston.

The singers were invited to become anchor tenants at New Massey Hall from the day the first plans were being drawn up in the 1970s. It certainly helped that then–Toronto Symphony Orchestra music director Andrew Davis was an enthusiastic proponent of choral music. The choir and its music director, Elmer Iseler, performed at the opening gala in 1982 and continued to be frequent occupants in Roy Thomson Hall's choir seats at the back of the stage, most notably for the annual December performances of Handel's *Messiah* with the Toronto Symphony Orchestra. During Iseler's time as the choir's conductor, he frequently led *Messiah* performances — as many as 150 in total over his tenure, according to *The Encyclopedia of Music in Canada*.

Thanks to its long working relationship with the Toronto Symphony Orchestra, the Toronto Mendelssohn Choir has been integral to most of the large-scale works for orchestra and choir in the classical repertoire presented at Roy Thomson Hall. The grandest of them all, Gustav Mahler's Symphony No. 8, also known as the *Symphony of a Thousand*, was presented twice under Andrew Davis in the 1980s and, most recently, during the 2011–12 season under current music director Peter Oundjian. Other epic works presented more than once over the past three decades have included Ralph Vaughan Williams's *A Sea Symphony*, Benjamin Britten's *War Requiem*, Leoš Janáček's *Glagolitic Mass*, and the concert requiems of Wolfgang Amadeus Mozart, Hector Berlioz, Johannes Brahms, and Giuseppe Verdi. Carl Orff's popular *Carmina Burana* has featured on many programs, but the favourite piece of all continues to be Ludwig van Beethoven's Symphony No. 9.

On occasion, the Toronto Symphony Orchestra has invited other city choirs to join it in concert at Roy Thomson Hall. Among the symphony's favourite young guests are the members of the Toronto Children's Chorus, founded by Jean Ashworth Bartle in 1978 at the request of conductor Davis, who needed treble voices for a performance of the *Nutcracker* ballet suite. Over the past thirty years, other choral guests have included the Toronto Bach Choir (now defunct), the Amadeus Choir and its professional core the Elmer Iseler Singers, the University of Toronto's MacMillan Singers, the Canadian Children's Opera Chorus, and the Bach Children's Chorus.

Although it was not the building's principal tenant, the Toronto Mendelssohn Choir probably made best use of the new building's rehearsal hall and the adjustable

The early rehearsal hall, with Elmer Iseler and the Toronto Mendelssohn Choir.

Courtesy of Inprint Editorial Services.

acoustics in the auditorium prior to the 2002 acoustical renovation. Much of the credit must go to Iseler, whose compulsive desire to make of the Toronto Mendelssohn Choir a world-class ensemble pushed him to use every means at his disposal to achieve that excellence. Whereas the Toronto Symphony Orchestra found the rehearsal hall too confining for large symphonic music, the two-storey room was a boon to the choristers, who had spent years rehearsing in a dingy rented space on Bloor Street. "Our old rehearsal space was so bad during the winter that we had to move everybody to the centre of the room because the wind came right through the windows and froze the women of the choir in their street clothes," Iseler recalled after the move to the choir's new home. The fact that the music library and a spacious dressing room and lounge were only steps away further added to the convenience and novelty of the freshly built headquarters in 1982.

Unlike others, who might have been intimidated by the hall's adjustable clear-acrylic discs and ceiling tubes, Iseler was keen to explore the possibilities of the variable acoustics to suit the choir's wide-ranging repertoire, which featured regular performances of the *St. Matthew* and *St. John Passions* of Johann Sebastian Bach, as well as premieres of new pieces by Canadian and international composers. "I was very glad we had an acoustical demonstration for the opening," the conductor told an interviewer at the time of Roy Thomson Hall's fifth anniversary, "because we were able to show off the flexibility of the hall right from the very beginning. I was concerned in conducting the premiere of R. Murray Schafer's *Sun*, a very complex composition, to have a rolling ambience. Then, when Andrew conducted [William Walton's] *Belshazzar's Feast*, we were able to tighten it slightly. I am sorry that over the years many conductors have forgotten about this acoustical flexibility. I remember when Krzysztof Penderecki came. He was worried and said, 'My music needs a cathedral sound.' So we changed the setting, flew the tubes and he said, 'Why is this not done all the time?'" The Toronto Mendelssohn Choir conductor soon realized that some acoustical configurations worked better than others, eventually establishing what became known to everyone in the building as the "Elmer Iseler setting."

While conductors may have forgotten about the flexibility of being able to adjust hundreds of those flying acoustical cylinders and fabric tubes, audiences may not have realized it at all. As Roy Thomson Hall's first production manager Pat Taylor recalled, the building team had originally intended to make the acoustical banners a part of each performance, having them begin their two-minute descent from the ceiling just before the start of a concert. But Taylor said this never happened because he was too busy with other things at that point. Instead, he would lower the banners before the doors were opened to admit the audience — a move that averted disaster in the one instance when the mechanism malfunctioned, sending a section of banners falling onto the seats below, two months after opening night.

Toronto Children's Chorus, with conductor and founder Jean Ashworth Bartle.

It was at Roy Thomson Hall that the Toronto Mendelssohn Choir celebrated its one hundredth birthday in 1984 — a date that coincided with Iseler's twentieth anniversary as the artistic director of the organization. The City of Toronto went so far as to declare November 3 to be Elmer Iseler Day, and, in a breathless news release, trumpeted "the distinguished achievements that this choral organization continues to set, with unprecedented standards of performance, unsurpassed in its magnificence of sound, remarkable clarity and expressive power." Two years later, the ensemble joined the Toronto Symphony Orchestra and Davis in their recording of *Messiah*. Released in the fall of 1987, the album went on to win a JUNO Award, and continues to be regarded as one of the best modern-instrument performances ever made of the famed oratorio. The Toronto Mendelssohn Choir also made its way into film, first singing some choral passages in *Agnes of God*, a 1985 movie starring Jane Fonda and made by Canadian director Norman Jewison. In 1993, the singers recorded choral passages in John Williams's score for the Steven Spielberg film, *Schindler's List*, a performance that went uncredited but brought a lot of satisfaction to members of the choir and Iseler at the end of his three-decade tenure as artistic director. Upon Iseler's death in April 1998, the musical commemoration of his life was fittingly held at Roy Thomson Hall — an event marked by companion choir concerts across the country. Due to a declining subscription base, the Toronto Mendelssohn Choir no longer holds its own concerts at Roy Thomson Hall, and is now an esteemed guest rather than a principal tenant.

One other individual had an important role in bringing choral music to Roy Thomson Hall: Nicholas Goldschmidt, one of the most significant figures in Canada's musical coming-of-age in the twentieth century. Niki, as he was known to anyone acquainted with him for more than five minutes, may have already been seventy-one by the time the new auditorium opened in 1982, but the indefatigable dreamer, planner, and organizer had more than two decades of musical projects intended for his adopted hometown, as well as other parts of the country, ahead of him. The long list of Toronto events included three international choral festivals

Elmer Iseler and Nicholas Goldschmidt.

Photo by Tom Sandler.

that included headline performances inside and outside of Arthur Erickson's concert venue — and the Roy Thomson Hall box office had the task of ticketing all three month-long events. Goldschmidt approached everything he did with a true enthusiast's zest, bringing along an international point of view that meant he treated Canadian artists and audiences as the equals of the world's most sophisticated.

Goldschmidt was born in 1908 in Moravia in the Czech Republic, not more than one hundred kilometres north of Vienna. He studied music in the Austrian capital alongside future conductor Herbert von Karajan — "We even played [piano] four hands and dated the same girl," he liked to tell interviewers. Steeped in opera and art song, the trained singer and composer could produce the words and music of any *lied* by Franz Schubert from memory, with little prompting. The multi-talented singer wasn't yet thirty when he decided to seek his professional fortune in North America. He immigrated to the United States in 1937 to direct opera programs at the San Francisco Conservatory and at nearby Stanford University. During the Second World War, he became director of the opera department at Columbia University in New York City before being lured to Toronto in order to become the first music director of the Royal Conservatory Opera School, which later became the Opera Division of the Faculty of Music at University of Toronto. This led to work as the first music director of the CBC Opera in the early days of television, and the music directorship of the Opera Festival Association, which gave birth to the Canadian Opera Company. His first major success in a pan-Canadian event came in his planning of Festival Canada in 1967, a nationwide project to celebrate the country's centennial in music.

The Toronto Mendelssohn Choir, with Noel Edison conducting.

Courtesy of Toronto Mendelssohn Choir.

Coming up with the International Choral Festival for Toronto in the late spring of 1989 was a huge undertaking, with the challenge of coordinating four thousand singers from twelve nations to present seventy concerts in thirty-five different venues — including Roy Thomson Hall and Metro Square (now David Pecaut Square). The gala opening concert, held at Roy Thomson Hall, assembled the Poliansky Choir from Moscow, the Obretenov Choir of Bulgaria, and Toronto's own boys of St. Michael's Choir School with the Toronto Symphony Orchestra under star Russian conductor Gennady Rozhdestvensky. The TSO was part of other concerts at the venue during the festival, including performances of Beethoven's *Missa Solemnis* with legendary American choral conductor Robert Shaw. The Montreal Symphony Orchestra came as well, to present Hector Berlioz's *Damnation of Faust* with music director Charles Dutoit. The Swiss conductor closed the festival with Giuseppe Verdi's *Requiem*, played by the TSO and sung by the Tanglewood Festival Chorus from the United States. The gala performances were all broadcast live by CBC Radio.

According to a *Globe and Mail* report at the time, sixty-five thousand people bought tickets to festival concerts and, despite a cost in excess of $3 million to organize and coordinate fees, travel, accommodations, and hall rentals, the festival achieved a $200,000 surplus, encouraging Goldschmidt and fellow organizers to plan a sequel. The next festival, which borrowed its title, "The Joy of Singing," from the inaugural event's logo, happened exactly four years later. It was even more ambitious, including more choirs from outside Europe and North America. There were eighty concerts, including the premiere of *Jezebel*, a new oratorio commissioned by the festival from Torontonians Robertson Davies, who supplied the text, and Derek Holman, who wrote the music. According to reports published at the time, the $800,000 in Roy Thomson Hall box office receipts were equal to the first festival's, but substantial cuts in government support brought on by a difficult economic recession in 1991–92 meant that the second event ended with a $250,000 deficit. Eventually the bills were all paid, and Goldschmidt organized one last big choral blowout two years before his death in February 2004: "The Joy of Singing within the Noise of the World." Like the other festivals, this last one again brought together top Canadian and international forces, but because of preparations for the acoustic renovation at Roy Thomson Hall, the big concerts were held at Massey Hall, where the Toronto Mendelssohn Choir had written the opening chapters of its history more than a century earlier.

Although Toronto's large choir festivals are now history, Roy Thomson Hall continues to host choral concerts. A favourite is the Mormon Tabernacle Choir of Salt Lake City (Roy Thomson himself was reportedly once a benefactor), which has appeared four times: in 1984, 1992, 2007, and 2011. As noted, the venue itself produces its own annual series of free lunchtime concerts featuring a visiting choir paired with the hall's Gabriel Kney organ.

In 1988 the Toronto musical event of the year was a performance by the Vienna Philharmonic, conducted by Leonard Bernstein. It was Bernstein's one and only appearance on the Roy Thomson Hall stage. He announced his retirement from conducting on October 9, 1990, and died of a heart attack five days later. He was seventy-two years old.

CHAPTER 7

Celebrating a World of Classical Guests

A S A PLACE where the paths of artists cross those of people who want to experience and appreciate their work, Roy Thomson Hall has welcomed hundreds of the world's very best classical instrumentalists and singers. Some were one-time visits, while others were preludes for return engagements. Over the course of three decades, there has been an ebb and flow to these visits, producing a bounty of concerts some seasons and fewer dates in others. The 1980s were a heyday for big-label classical recordings, a phenomenon that boosted active international touring schedules. North Americans pulled back a bit in the 1990s, while young performers, as well as audiences, in East Asia confidently took to the Western classical canon. By the end of the first decade of the twenty-first century, the classical world was furiously adapting to listeners sharing music digitally for free, dealing with the explosion of social media, and trying to understand how young audiences could be enticed to sample the pleasures of art music in the context of the traditional concert setting.

As Roy Thomson Hall's programmers look forward to their next thirty years, it's not at all clear how the presentation of classical artists is going to evolve. But that takes nothing away from the fact that the city's music lovers can look back on three decades gilded with memorable visits by the world's great orchestras, singers, and solo instrumentalists.

It is no accident that the most famous artists have often been the ones to return the most often. More than a generation has passed since legendary singers such as Lois Marshall, Maureen Forrester, Dame Kiri Te Kanawa, Leontyne Price,

A birthday celebration.

Soprano Renée Fleming with Nada Ristich of BMO Financial Group, and sopranos Virginia Hatfield, Shannon Mercer, and Gillian Grossman, 2012.

Photo by Jag Gundu.

Marilyn Horne, Elly Ameling, and Nicolai Gedda first graced the Roy Thomson Hall stage. Because they were all present during the opening season, audiences quickly learned to expect the highest of artistic standards when they came through the glass doors on Simcoe Street. But even the prestigious International Vocal Recitals series couldn't weather shrinking audiences, presenting its final season in 2009–10.

Two women whose remarkable artistry never fails to draw crowds to the circular auditorium, however, are American soprano Renée Fleming and Italian mezzo-soprano Cecilia Bartoli. No two divas could be more different in style and attitude as they turn on the musical fireworks — Fleming is all elegant poise, while Bartoli vibrates with energy — but they share a special charisma that Torontonians have been able to follow from early promise right through to superstardom. *Globe and Mail* music critic Robert Everett-Green enthused how Bartoli "tore the roof off Toronto's Roy Thomson Hall" during her February 1993 debut, labelling her "the mezzo of dreams." Not quite five years later, after another sold-out visit, critic Urjo Kareda put his analytical finger on the singer's secret: "Cecilia Bartoli's ability to make her audiences feel the beauty of the music she sings in an almost tactile way is what sends them into a frenzy." Critiquing one of Fleming's recitals, in April 2004, Everett-Green concluded that "the ancient idea of majesty is that its very presence exalts, and American soprano Renée Fleming lived every inch up to the regal billing," adding that she "sang like an angel."

Men were equally capable of drawing praise from critics and audiences alike. Welsh bass-baritone Bryn Terfel has been the embodiment of affable charm in four solo concerts since his Toronto debut in 1996. Russian baritone Dmitri Hvorostovsky has excelled in both art song and operatic recitals. A sentimental Canadian favourite, tenor Ben Heppner has also walked upon the stage's maple boards multiple times. He participated in the storied "Millennium Opera Gala" of December 31, 1999 — a night that signalled the Roy Thomson Hall debuts of several young singers who would become regular performers there during the first decade of the twenty-first century. His most recent shining moment was as a soloist with La Scala Philharmonic in 2007, part of Roy Thomson Hall's twenty-fifth anniversary gala.

There have been many notable names affixed to the dressing room doors over the years. South Korean coloratura soprano Sumi Jo attracted a whole new audience for each of her three spectacular shows of vocal agility. And the Roy Thomson Hall stage was an integral part of the rise of Canadian sopranos Measha Brueggergosman and Isabel Bayrakdarian, who were brought into the spotlight at the "Millennium Opera Gala." Polish contralto Ewa Podles, hired several times by Canadian Opera Company general director Richard Bradshaw, was a less frequent guest at King and Simcoe Streets, but left a deep imprint when Bradshaw and the Toronto Symphony Orchestra accompanied her in a concert that included Gioacchino Rossini's *Giovanna d'Arco*, in May 2007. "Had the real Joan of Arc sung like Podles, her enemies would have spontaneously combusted," read the John Terauds review in the *Toronto Star*. She returned one more time the following year to sing a solo recital. "Podles pulled out all the stops in her great organ of a voice," wrote Ken Winters in the *Globe and Mail*, remarking that "the audience was swept away."

Two Canadian powerhouses have thrilled audiences several times in recent memory: soprano Karina Gauvin, who grew up in Toronto, and Quebec contralto Marie-Nicole Lemieux. They were introduced to Roy Thomson Hall by a visiting orchestra from Quebec, Les Violons du Roy. All instantly became favourite guests. As critic Tamara Bernstein declared after an April 2007 concert, "The sheer beauty of both singers' voices was matched by their thrilling, mature artistry."

We would be remiss to turn to the highlights of orchestral visits without mentioning Salute to Vienna, which, since its inaugural concert in 1995, has become an annual New Year's Day tradition in a city otherwise recovering from holiday festivities. Produced by Attila and Marion Glatz, the program's heady mix of waltzes and operetta excerpts is a direct homage to the New Year's concert that has been a fixture in Vienna since 1939. This has brought a dash of Old World élan to Arthur Erickson's modern temple to the performing arts, much as the Vienna Philharmonic Orchestra has, having graced the stage on seven occasions.

The illustrious Austrians' first performance at Roy Thomson Hall in November 1988 was particularly memorable not only for its quality, but also for its effort to bridge the divide between Old and New Worlds, thanks to the presence of Leonard Bernstein on the podium. The American icon had not appeared in Toronto since the mid-1960s, and such was the buzz around the city that a long line of fans waited along Simcoe Street in fervent yet ultimately vain hope that some tickets would magically turn up for the sold-out concert. In his *Globe* review, Everett-Green sympathized with the many who had been left out on the sidewalk that evening, writing, "They missed a rare display of what can still be done with the medium of the symphony orchestra, and of what distinction of style can still be retained in the age of the recording." Roy Thomson Hall president Edward Pickering, the man who had pushed so hard for this new concert space and then guided it through its first seven seasons, crowned the occasion by announcing his retirement with a bow on stage before the start of the music.

Like the Vienna Philharmonic Orchestra, the Royal Concertgebouw Orchestra of Amsterdam also came to town seven times between 1982 and 2002. In the company of conductor Riccardo Chailly, the Dutch musicians could not have pleased the *Toronto Star*'s William Littler any more. "There is simply no such thing as overexposure to the kind of music-making this ensemble represents," he wrote in the *Star* after a concert in February 1999. "In orchestral terms, music-making just doesn't get much better." Three seasons later, Littler celebrated the 2002 Concertgebouw concert as one of the year's highlights, at the same time lamenting that this would be its final visit with Chailly on the podium.

Fortunately for fans of symphonic repertoire, Russian conductor Valery Gergiev and the ensemble now known as the Mariinsky Orchestra handily stepped into the breach left by the Dutch in 2001. Their electric interpretations of twentieth-century Russian music — sometimes presented in two separate programs over two nights — became highly anticipated events during Roy Thomson Hall's third decade. "Toronto is not a city accustomed to hearing many visiting orchestras, and few cities anywhere can expect to experience music-making at this level on a day-to-day basis," wrote Littler in the *Star* after two consecutive nights of the then–Kirov Orchestra in April 2005.

Valery Gergiev, conductor of the Mariinsky Orchestra, talks with former governor general of Canada Adrienne Clarkson (right) and other guests at the 2010 gala.

Photo by Tom Sandler.

A double whammy of rising costs and declining government funding for touring orchestra concerts has caused a sharp decline in visits by large ensembles in most North American cities since the late 1990s. The situation was made more acute in the aftermath of the terrorist attacks of September 11, 2001, and consequent work-permit complexities and frequent quibbles with security and airline personnel over bringing instruments on board. In the 2012–13 season, for example, Roy Thomson Hall hosted but a single international ensemble, the Vienna Philharmonic Orchestra. But Toronto did enjoy a rare burst of multinational orchestral colour during the 2009–10 season, when five international groups came calling: the Cleveland Orchestra, in October 2009; the Shanghai Symphony Orchestra the following month — a concert that introduced the audience to Yuja Wang, the latest young Chinese artist to light up the piano world; the Rotterdam Philharmonic Orchestra with new Canadian music director Yannick Nézet-Séguin in February 2010; Gergiev and the Mariinsky Orchestra with two programs in March; and superstar Chinese pianist Lang Lang and the Schleswig-Holstein Festival Orchestra under conductor Christoph Eschenbach in April.

As noted earlier, no history of classical music in Canada is complete without mention of Nicholas Goldschmidt, the Czech émigré who worked tirelessly to enrich concert life in Toronto and parts beyond from his arrival in 1946 right up to his death at age ninety-five in 2004. The three international choir festivals he organized have been described. But there were two other notable festivals masterminded by Goldschmidt that encompassed the city, Roy Thomson Hall, and its box office. The first was a festival honouring the three hundredth anniversary, in 1985, of the birth of Johann Sebastian Bach. Woven into the programming was a one-time International Bach Piano Competition. It was this contest, whose jury included French composer Olivier Messiaen and his pianist wife Yvonne Loriod, that confirmed Ottawa-born Angela Hewitt as one of the most important young talents of her generation. Her final performance, earning first prize, was captured for the whole country to watch and hear by the CBC, live from Roy Thomson Hall. As Hewitt recalls, "For ten years, since the age of sixteen, I had been on the international piano competition circuit, winning many prizes but lacking the 'big one.' Winning this would, I knew, launch me worldwide and put an end to competitions for life." And it did.

The CBC — in particular its second radio network, once known as CBC Stereo — was very much a part of the musical story at Roy Thomson Hall, especially

Angela Hewitt, winner of the 1985 International Bach Piano Competition: "When I walk out on stage of Roy Thomson Hall, I think of the night of May 10, 1985, when it was packed to the rafters for the finals of the competition. What an atmosphere! What an audience! May the excitement live on."

in the early years, when the public broadcaster saw the venue as Canada's answer to Carnegie Hall, a place where the best and the brightest would congregate to celebrate homegrown and international talent. It helped that the venue's first general manager, William Armstrong, had been plucked from the management ranks of the CBC. "I think he played a big role in connecting the CBC with this new venture," recalled Eric Friesen, who hosted *Live from Roy Thomson Hall* on CBC Stereo during the first two seasons. "Right from the beginning, Bill was on this charge that broadcasting had to be a key part of the hall's mission, that the CBC audience was to be a part of the hall's audience." Friesen also believed that hearing the world's finest artists live from the country's biggest city might also help with civic public relations: "If you're sitting in Regina and you hate Toronto, the fact that you can hear Claudio Arrau live is still a big bloody deal. The true music lover would tell you what a thrill it is to be there."

Ronald Osborne, chair of the Board of Governors, 2008–10, at the 2010 gala.

Photo by Tom Sandler.

That thrill was present in the late spring of 1991, when Goldschmidt unveiled a month-long musical celebration of the two hundredth anniversary of the death of Wolfgang Amadeus Mozart. With Roy Thomson Hall at its epicentre, but also involving the renovated Elgin and Winter Garden Theatres, among other downtown venues, the festival celebrated the wunderkind eighteenth-century Austrian composer with orchestral and chamber music, in song, opera, and dance. A series of international competitions was held across Canada, with finale concerts taking place in Toronto. The festival opened with a solo recital by Dutch soprano Elly Ameling at Roy Thomson Hall. Other estimable musical guests included conductor Helmuth Rilling and the Beaux Arts Trio. In an inspired act of community inclusiveness, seven hundred young students of the Royal Conservatory of Music celebrated the creations of a young Mozart on the big stage.

CHAPTER 8

The Art of Making Music Sound Good

DESPITE THE JOY brought to thousands of audience members by the fine music-making at Roy Thomson Hall, the chorus of criticism about the quality of sound inside the concert space started as discreet murmurs within months of its doors being opened to the public. The gripes gradually grew in a crescendo, despite multiple tweaks and adjustments to Theodore Schultz's finely tuned acoustic machinery. What its dreamers and builders had envisaged as an acoustic marvel had turned out to be far less than perfect. These maladies resulted in a large-scale renovation of the hall's interior in 2002, euphemistically labelled as an "enhancement project."

To understand what was wrong with the acoustics of Roy Thomson Hall and how most of these problems were resolved in 2002, it is helpful to know a little bit about the art and the science of how sound is transmitted and diffused. Two people need to work together in designing a concert auditorium: an architect and an acoustician. Both professions are based on years of study involving the relationships between structure and open space. Both involve work with abstract concepts as well as physical realities, often using complex mathematical formulas. But while most architects think of themselves as artists first, acousticians refer to themselves as men and women of science. An unspoken assumption in the modern world is that when someone invokes scientific study and applications, they are basing their work on incontrovertible fact, on theories proven in both the laboratory and the real world. But an acoustical engineer designing a concert space employs both art and science.

On November 16, 2000, Roy Thomson Hall unveiled the Enhancement Project. Helping saw the first plank was Linda Campbell; the Honourable David Collenette, federal minister for the GTA; and Thomas Payne, partner of KPMB Architects.

The science of acoustics goes back as far as the Roman Empire, which built amphitheatres that successfully transmitted the human voice and music to thousands of spectators without the benefit of full walls, a ceiling, or any sort of amplification. The father of modern acoustical analysis for concert spaces is American physicist Wallace Sabine (1868–1919), whose mathematical formula linking reverberation time to the size of a room and the amount of sound it can absorb was so compelling that he was asked to be a consultant in the design and construction of Symphony Hall in Boston six years after Massey Hall opened its doors. The New England landmark continues to set the modern standard for fine acoustics. As the famous twentieth-century British conductor Sir Adrian Boult said, "The ideal concert hall is obviously that into which you make a not very pleasant sound and the audience received something that is quite beautiful. I maintain that this really can happen in Boston Symphony Hall; it is our ideal."

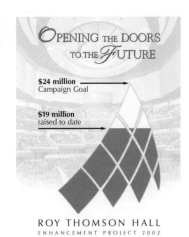

Large lobby signs showed ongoing campaign progress.

That building is based on the classic shoebox model — like the Musikverein in Vienna or the Concertgebouw in Amsterdam — that was the tried-and-true vessel for classical concerts until after the Second World War. Boston's Symphony Hall seats 2,625 people, only five fewer than Roy Thomson Hall in its current state. But acousticians grew cocky in brandishing their reverberation formulae, emboldening them to toy with the size and shape of interiors as long as the theoretical numbers kept adding up. Roy Thomson Hall acoustician Theodore Schultz, coincidentally a Bostonian with a Ph.D. in acoustics from Harvard University, was considered to be one of the most accomplished practitioners in the field at the time. He was also a modern man of science who thought he could work wonders with shapes and sizes never previously used in presenting live classical music. But, despite a professional resumé boasting numerous high-profile projects around the world, the man of science was not beyond using techniques anyone could try at home to visualize his acoustical goals. Roy Thomson Hall's first production manager, Pat Taylor, vividly recalled accompanying Schultz into the dark hall, where he was asked to shine a beam of light onto walls that the acoustician had covered with reflective material so that he could observe how the light was reflected back into the auditorium. "He believed that sound travelled like light," Taylor said.

Toronto architect Jack Diamond, who would later design the Four Seasons Centre for the Performing Arts, was one of the few onlookers who was not convinced that New Massey Hall was going to live up to its acoustical potential. He criticized the building's plans publicly in a *Toronto Star* interview in February 1979, calling the venue "entirely the wrong shape for a concert hall." He explained that "there is no mystery to acoustics. Sound behaves in an entirely predictable fashion. If you have a flat surface, the sound reflects. If you have a concave surface it concentrates the sound like a lens. The orchestra can't hear itself play and

Top left: All construction equipment, including components of the three cranes, needed to be no larger than the stage wing doors, which measure nine feet high by eight-and-one-half feet wide.

Top right: The organ remained wrapped throughout the construction.

Bottom: Charles Cutts and Marcia Lewis Brown, chair of the Board of Governors, 2001–03.

Photos by Cliff Spicer.

the audience can't hear the orchestra." These observations turned out to be remarkably accurate, but it was hard to argue with the momentum around the New Massey Hall architectural design imperatives.

Edward Pickering, who championed the campaign for New Massey Hall, didn't want a conventional concert box because it meant that some members of the audience would have a more intimate relationship with the performers than others, something he considered elitist. While Roy Thomson Hall was being built, Arthur Erickson recalled how Pickering also disdained straight lines "that you never find in nature." Working together, Schultz and Erickson came up with thirty-two models for New Massey Hall, all designed to wrap the audience around the stage as much as possible, before settling on an acceptable compromise of size, sight lines, intimate feel, and quality of sound.

As is so often the case, this same spirit of humanizing and democratizing the concert hall was sweeping the world in the 1970s. Schultz found himself designing other music venues with a similar mandate, including Louise M. Davies Symphony Hall in San Francisco and Melbourne Concert Hall (now known as Hamer Hall) in Australia. All three venues boasted an open plan where the stage was not set behind a proscenium arch but included in the main, high-ceiling volume of the auditorium. To help focus the sound and reflect part of it back down to the musicians so that they would be able to hear themselves play, Schultz specified clouds of adjustable, clear acrylic discs above the stage. The hall in Melbourne opened the same year as Toronto's, but San Francisco's building had already been open for two seasons and was already becoming the subject of the kind of criticism from performers and patrons — for lifeless, dry sound — that would soon plague Roy Thomson Hall's first two decades. The volume of each of these three venues was simply too large, causing the intensity of sound to weaken noticeably before it reached the ears of many audience members. In the case of Roy Thomson Hall, interior volume was two-thirds greater than that of Massey Hall, despite containing a similar number of seats. Besides making some concerts less captivating, orchestra musicians had to work harder to make music, increasing wear and tear on their bodies and instruments.

Acoustical rigour had been misdirected in this case. As acoustical experts Trevor Cox and Peter D'Antonio wrote in "Engineering Art: The Science of Concert Hall Acoustics" in the June 2003 edition of *Interdisciplinary Science Reviews*, "Modern acoustic science cannot guarantee a great acoustic every time, but if advice is followed, technical knowledge should ensure that bad halls are not built, while significantly increasing the chance of greatness being achieved." In a 2012 report on the state of science in the design of concert halls, Norwegian acoustician Magne Skalevik wrote that there can still be a huge gap between what measuring instruments and mathematical formulas say, and what the listener's ear perceives, leading him to believe that "this paradox calls for open-minded exploration of the link between physical stimulus and listeners' subjective response."

Although they could have waited for science to evolve, San Franciscans were the first to act, approving a $10-million renovation of Louise M. Davies Hall, completed in 1992. That project became the template for the work that would be done in Toronto a decade later, and that was finished in Melbourne's Hamer Hall in 2012. Schultz had died suddenly in 1989, which compelled the operators of all three halls to go elsewhere for expertise.

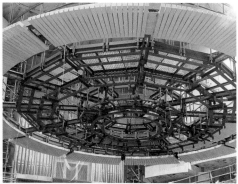

The acoustic canopies were built off-site, disassembled, and then reassembled in the auditorium.

Photos by Cliff Spicer.

Soon after Schultz's death, John Lawson, who had succeeded Pickering as president and CEO in 1988, formed an acoustic selection committee, chaired by Peter Hertzberg, long-time chair of the hall's property committee. The committee, which included TSO representation, interviewed a number of acousticians, ultimately engaging Russell Johnson and his firm Artec Consultants Inc. of New York City in 1990. Johnson and Artec had emerged as the pre-eminent voices in concert hall design in the 1980s. Lawson had visited a great number of international concert halls alone or on tour with the TSO and the Toronto Mendelssohn Choir, including a guided tour by Johnson himself of the new Birmingham Hall. Artec's initial report in 1991, by Russell Johnson and his associate Bob Essert, recommended a program of studies that was extensive and costly. It was put on hold to the disappointment of all, particularly the TSO.

Shortly after taking over as president and CEO in 1992, Charles Cutts reviewed the acoustic history and met with Russell Johnson and Bob Essert to re-examine

Ken Thomson and Jukka-Pekka Saraste, TSO music director, 2000.

the options. Due to a $1-million positive turnaround in operations and a plan to reach $10 million in reserves by 2000, the board agreed that the acoustics should be revisited. In 1994, Artec sent a revised proposal suggesting ten ways that Roy Thomson Hall could be made to sound better. Johnson recommended that they all be implemented at once, rather than in piecemeal fashion. The board approved the project, which involved getting detailed quotes from architects and contractors, as well as raising the required money. In the end only two of those ten fixes were not implemented in the final enhancement project, which came in at a cost of $20 million. The work was supposed to go ahead in 2000, but was instead moved back two years because, among other things, various construction-trade contract negotiations were coming up, and the board wanted to ensure there would be no delays to jeopardize a concert season.

The first item not addressed in the final enhancement plan involved fitting the stage with hydraulic risers, but the Toronto Symphony Orchestra was in bad financial shape and its music director Jukka-Pekka Saraste left in 2001, which made it an inopportune time to consider such a big change to how the orchestra would look and function on stage. The other Artec recommendation to fall by the wayside was a change to the profile of the hall's balcony facades. Besides the extra expense, it would have further irritated Arthur Erickson, who was unhappy that he had not been included in the planning and design for changes to his landmark building. Instead of Erickson, the design work went to Thomas Payne of Toronto firm KPMB Architects. EllisDon would manage the execution.

Project team meetings included staff from KPMB Architects, Artec, EllisDon, and Roy Thomson Hall.

As had been the case in San Francisco and Melbourne, the main remedy involved reducing the volume of the hall so that sound energy would be stronger for the audience. KPMB and Artec specified twenty-three wooden bulkheads around the top perimeter of the auditorium and wooden partitions at the back of the orchestra seating level. These new structures reduced the interior space from nearly 28,000 cubic metres to approximately 24,000 cubic metres (still 5,700 cubic metres more than Massey Hall's volume). These pieces would be pre-built elsewhere to minimize construction time inside the building. Instead of bare concrete and cut-pile carpeting, the new walls and the floors were lined with Canadian maple — four thousand square metres of it — which is good at reflecting sound and which would bring a dash of warmth to the cool-grey space. The job of focusing sound coming from the stage was largely assigned to an acoustic canopy made up of two round, concentric structures adjustable in height, and weighing a total of thirty-eight tonnes. These, too, were finished in maple and fitted with rectangular onyx light fixtures. Behind the ceiling and walls, the ventilation and electrical systems were upgraded to reduce noise.

Erickson, who had already described the removal of a portion of the acoustic tubes from Roy Thomson Hall's ceiling in 1983 as "a desecration," went on a public-relations offensive in 2001. "I know when people see it, they'll be just horrified," he told the *National Post* when the enhancement project was unveiled. In response, Thomas Payne called the use of wood "an expressive decision. It's an interpretation of a situation, and an impulse to create something that will be successful behind anything else that might be done." Erickson, looking for an advocate, wrote a letter to Ken Thomson in which he pleaded that "the changes brashly destroy the aesthetic quality of the interiors." He then wrote a similar letter that was published in Thomson's newspaper, the *Globe and Mail*, in which he added that the hall's cool-grey aesthetic had been praised by such internationally respected musicians as Cecilia Bartoli and Leonard Bernstein. On the other hand, Cutts recalled how, during a visit with the Vienna Philharmonic orchestra in 1993, conductor Sir Georg Solti had suggested that the auditorium would benefit from the warmth of wood.

While much of this work was designed to improve the quality of acoustic concerts, amplified sound would see improvements as well. The acoustic canopy includes a state-of-the-art speaker cluster as well as stage lighting, and the bulkheads house retractable acoustic banners that help produce the less reverberant acoustic necessary for clean amplified sound. And all audiences would be able to appreciate the creation of two wide aisles and a series of side boxes to replace the former "continental" seating arrangement on the main floor that required audience members to work their way awkwardly to centre seats from far away. The renovation subtly altered the auditorium's shape from circular to more rectangular, while reducing seating capacity by 182 places, from 2,812 to 2,630.

The $20-million renovation budget was covered by a balance of private fundraising and the corporation's cash reserves. The fundraising campaign, ably co-chaired by former board chairs John Clappison and Patsy Anderson, was managed by director of marketing and development Heather Clark. The campaign raised $13 million, which included a lead donation of $5 million from The Woodbridge Company Limited, the holding company of the Thomson family. Ken Thomson, whose original gift had prompted New

Left: John Clappison, chair of the Board of Governors, 1997–99.

Right: Patsy Anderson, chair of the Board of Governors, 1999–2001, at the enhancement project press conference, 2000.

The North Court, as seen
in the fall of 2002.

Photo by Richard Beland.

Massey Hall to be named after his father, was initially skeptical regarding the scope
of the project, but came around after he was shown all the details of what would
be done — and how it could be accomplished within very strict financial and time
parameters. In the brochure that was sent to prospective donors, he wrote, "The
Thomson family is pleased to invest in a great new era of cultural excellence at
one of North America's most active and popular concert venues. Our family is
extremely proud of this Hall, which bears my father's name."

At the last minute, an infrastructure project announced by Ottawa and Queen's
Park brought in an extra $4 million of public money that allowed the corporation
to rework the old rehearsal hall by reducing its ceiling height and, in the process,
create room for a spacious donors' lounge — officially opened in the spring of 2004.

Although Cutts enjoys the critical accolades that Roy Thomson Hall received
after the renovation, he remains particularly proud of how this substantial and
complicated work could be completed with only twenty-two weeks of shutdown
time, from March 10 to August 13, 2002. "I promised Ken Thomson that we would
do this on time and on budget," says Cutts of a bargain kept.

The project could not have been done on time and on budget without the
exceptional construction team, which included Susan Jegins, the hall's long-serving vice-president of operations and administration; Bill Conley, building services
manager; Tom Payne and David Jesson of KPMB; Steve Seifert, vice-president of

engineering at EllisDon; and Aldo Palma, of the property committee. Jegins was guided throughout by Bill Neish, retired principal of NORR Architects and chair of the board's property committee. "It was the right team on both sides," said Neish, "and that doesn't always happen."

In the end, even Erickson acquiesced, in a qualified way. Cutts tells the story of how late one Friday afternoon in August 2002 Erickson called from the airport to say he was coming over to see the building. "I decided I'd meet him at the front doors," Cutts recalls. "Then I walked him backstage and out onto the stage. His very first words were, 'Wow, that's impressive.' Then, for the next forty-five minutes, he tore apart the hall, about the wood and all that kind of stuff. But I had that one moment when I knew we had done the right thing."

After being warmed up by Toronto International Film Festival stars and audiences earlier in the month, Roy Thomson Hall was officially reopened with a gala concert on September 21, 2002, led, as it had been twenty years earlier, by the Toronto Symphony Orchestra and its conductor laureate Sir Andrew Davis. The celebration featured the Toronto Children's Chorus, the Toronto Mendelssohn Choir, Measha Brueggergosman, and James Ehnes. Bass-baritone Nathan Berg was the soloist in Walton's *Belshazzar's Feast* — the same oratorio that had opened the building in 1982. Davis stepped off the podium to pay homage to the Toronto Symphony Orchestra's great conductor from Massey Hall days, Sir Ernest MacMillan, playing his *Cortège Académique* on the re-voiced Gabriel Kney organ. The *Toronto Star* awarded Roy Thomson Hall an editorial-page laurel the following

Roy Thomson Hall reopening, September 2002, with the Toronto Symphony Orchestra, the Toronto Mendelssohn Choir, conductor Andrew Davis, and soloists.

Photo by Richard Beland.

day, "for passing with top marks the first public test of its $20-million acoustical renovation." Critic Tamara Bernstein, writing in the *National Post*, enthused that "Artec Consultants Inc., the most respected acoustic firm in the world, has transmuted the hall's leaden acoustics into something that sounds an awful lot like gold. The $20-million renovation to Roy Thomson Hall seems to have worked."

Both art and science had, for once, triumphed.

Davis, looking back over his experience on the podium, first at Massey Hall, at Roy Thomson Hall in its original iteration, and then after the enhancement project, admits that he liked the new building in 1982, "but I always felt that the new hall was better for classical things and complex works such as Stravinsky's *Rite of Spring*. It really fell down in music by Brahms and Bruckner, where you want the hall to assist with resonance."

He believes that reducing the interior volume of the auditorium in 2002 was a significant factor in improving its acoustics. "It was certainly easier to hear on stage than we had anticipated and we had an adjustable canopy overhead. We fiddled around with it but didn't adjust it too often. We settled on a standard setting," Davis recalls. "It is now more than just good; it is very good."

CHAPTER 9

Broad Programming Is All About Community

CLASSICAL PROGRAMMING AND the acoustical challenges it sometimes faced at Roy Thomson Hall dominated daily arts pages in newspapers over the first two decades of the building's history. However, this story only touched upon the issue of designing programs to mirror a diverse city with many different audiences, encompassing a broad range of styles and cultures. In a memorandum written a year before the new building opened, Edward Pickering reminded the board of governors that "our mandate is to offer facilities to a family of users ... [and] to cater to all forms of music, from symphonic to rock, to western and jazz." As with so many of his wishes, Pickering was a man of his word.

A look through three decades of entries in Roy Thomson Hall's guest book reveals how its lineup of visiting artists has evolved in much the same way that audiences change from generation to generation. The venue's celebratory opening weeks included concerts by Canadian legends Anne Murray and Gordon Lightfoot as well as Sharon, Lois & Bram. Musical comedian Anna Russell came by, while Liza Minnelli spent four full nights on the stage. An unlikely duo of mugging comedians, the veteran Buddy Hackett with newcomer Jim Carrey, left fans in stitches in February 1983, heralding the arrival of more laughs from Don Rickles and George Carlin later in the spring. Meanwhile, the Smithsonian Jazz Repertory Ensemble and Keith Jarrett brought out Toronto's jazz aficionados to the biggest and glitziest dive in town. Pop vocalist Sheena Easton was but twenty-three years old, in the full bloom of her James Bond–fuelled fame, when she came to unleash a bit of summer vocal magic to close that golden first season.

Backstage at Roy Thomson Hall: June Carter Cash, Bob Dylan, Carlene Carter (June's daughter), and Johnny Cash. Dylan has performed at Massey Hall, and Johnny Cash performed at both Massey Hall and Roy Thomson Hall.

The common threads in this variety pack of performers were quality and name recognition, two attributes that apply to all types of programming carried out at Roy Thomson Hall since the earliest days. The mix of genres has changed quite a bit, though. One only has to look at some of the repeat visitors in the first decade to see the passing of styles as one era gives way to the next. The Glenn Miller Orchestra and waltz king Lawrence Welk's soap-bubbly ballroom band were colourful draws to Arthur Erickson's grey-on-grey concert space for people born in the early years of the twentieth century. Fans of folk and roots sounds came numerous times to catch visits by the Chieftains and the Irish Rovers. Actor George Clooney's aunt Rosemary, singer of jazz-inflected pop, was a popular draw. The Roy Thomson stage wasn't too fancy for Johnny Cash, nor too square for Johnny Mathis, Engelbert Humperdinck, or the heartthrobs of the double-knit pant-suit generation: singers Tom Jones and Cleo Laine. Other favourite pop artists, returning multiple times from points local as well as global, have included Rita MacNeil, Roger Whittaker, Burl Ives, Nana Mouskouri, and the Queen of Soul, the indomitable Aretha Franklin. As luck would have it, one of the original adult-contemporary masters, Tony Bennett, has defied generational divides as well as the passage of time and remains a favourite of visitors to the hall.

Each performer likes to leave his or her own stamp on a venue, but some stand out. For Roy Thomson Hall's first production manager Pat Taylor, one particularly vivid memory remains from Keith Jarrett's first visit. The jazz pianist's contract stated that he get a Steinway piano, of which there are always two ready for stage

Artistic director Muriel Sherrin and senior producer Pat Taylor, 1991.

Photo by Paul J. Hoeffler.

duty at Roy Thomson Hall. Both were waiting for him; he played both, chose one and, as he walked off the stage, noticed another concert grand in the wings. "He asked me, 'What's that?' I said, 'Oh, that's Glenn Gould's old Yamaha. It's not in the best of condition,'" Taylor recalled. "Jarrett walked up to it, pulled back the cover, opened it up and played it for a while. He then got on top of it and lay down for at least two minutes. He came off the piano and said, 'I'll play this one,' and I had to scramble to find the tuner." Since then, Glenn Gould's Yamaha CFII concert grand piano has been ready and available for concert duty in the Roy Thomson Hall lobby. Its last trip beyond King and Simcoe Streets came in 2012, first for a major refurbishing by

1997–98 season brochure cover.

Yamaha, followed by a star turn on the Convocation Hall stage in honour of what would have been Glenn Gould's eightieth birthday.

The hall has welcomed all sorts of non-musical headliners over the years as well. The roster of funny people to grace the stage has also followed generational tastes, starting with names like Red Skelton in 1989, who had translated early radio fame into the new medium of television in the 1950s. Borscht-belt comic Jackie Mason was there in the hall's early days too. The Smothers Brothers first appeared on the stage in 1988, and were followed by Bob Newhart, Bill Cosby, and upstarts Jay Leno and Whoopi Goldberg in more recent years.

Although equipped with audiovisual equipment to handle amplified concerts and spoken presentations, some acoustical tweaking became necessary early on, just as it had been necessary for unamplified classical concerts. Following Liza Minnelli's Roy Thomson Hall debut, general manager Geoffrey Butler realized that sound and lighting would need to be upgraded if the hall was going to cater successfully to pop acts. The lighting rig was simple enough to adjust, and with some experimentation, production manager Pat Taylor — who later became director of programming — found an ideal positioning for the hall's eight hundred acoustic banners. An updated sound system and the addition of several banks of speakers in early 1987 ensured that the hall was well equipped for what Taylor called the "big sound" of amplified concerts.

A poolside concert during the 1988 Downtown Jazz Festival.

Photo by Jim Galloway.

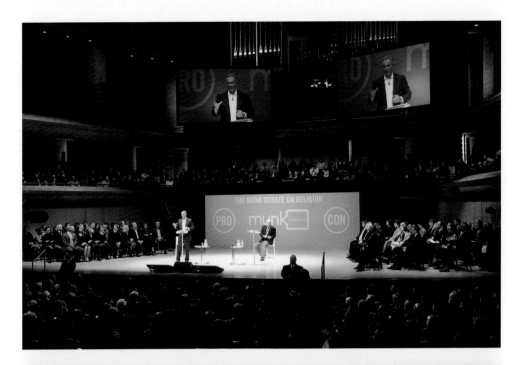

Tony Blair and Christopher Hitchens debate "Be it resolved, religion is a force for good in the world" at a Munk Debate, 2010.

Peter Munk, Brian Mulroney, and Henry Kissinger at a Munk Debate, "Be it resolved, the 21st century will belong to China," 2011.

Photos by Tom Sandler.

Ravi Shankar, who pioneered the rise of world music as a mainstage concert draw for the Beatles generation, was also no stranger to Toronto, drawing a pan-cultural audience to the city's premier stage over the course of many repeat appearances. The explosion of interest in the music of Cuba and the Buena Vista Social Club brought those legends, led by Ibrahim Ferrer, to the city in 1990 — first to Massey Hall, continuing with several repeat visits to Roy Thomson Hall.

The opening of the city's ears to more international sounds was a phenomenon that Wende Cartwright, who began a six-year stint as director of programming in 1994, wanted to strengthen. Cartwright — eager, in her words, to "mix it up" — set about engaging more communities in the Greater Toronto Area and making Roy Thomson Hall a more welcoming place. The people she met and spoke with in various multicultural communities were pleased by the prospect of seeing more world music performers on the hall's stage, and soon Roy Thomson Hall began co-presenting performances with a variety of cultural groups. Many international ensembles became favourites with return engagements at both venues, including Mazowsze (Poland's state Folk Song and Dance Ensemble), Peking Acrobats, Cesaria Evora, Kodo Drummers, and the Whirling Dervishes.

During the 1990s, Roy Thomson Hall was able to capitalize on grassroots work being performed in Toronto by people like Alan Davis and Jane Bunnett, as well as tap the growing pool of audiences from Toronto's South Asian and East Asian communities, to offer mainstage opportunities to artists with high profiles

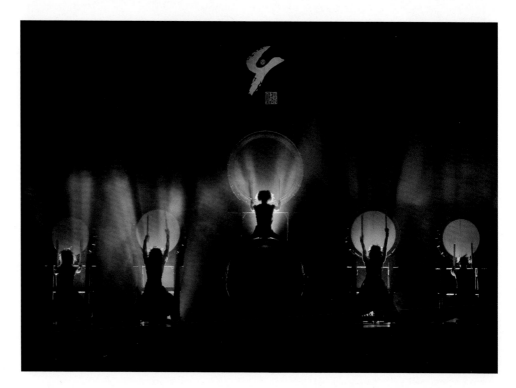

Yamato — The Drummers of Japan appeared at Roy Thomson Hall in 2005 and 2007.

Courtesy of Yamato – The Drummers of Japan.

Buffy Sainte-Marie at Unique Lives and Experiences, 2010.

Photo by Doug Sturgeon.

Massed Military Band Spectacular, an annual presentation of the Royal Canadian Military Institute.

in other parts of the world. Not only was this good for community building, it was good for the box office as well. During the second half of the 1990s, Roy Thomson Hall introduced and welcomed such talents as the Hong Kong Chinese Orchestra, Mehr and Sher Ali, the late Indian ghazal legend Jagjit Singh, the Veriovka Ukrainian Song and Dance Company, King Sunny Adé, and Cantonese pop diva Paula Tsui.

Having different kinds of performers on stage has necessarily entailed drawing audiences with different attitudes and levels of engagement. At a 1996 show by Pakistani devotional singer Nusrat Fateh Ali Khan, audience engagement took a dramatic turn when one especially ardent fan became so caught up in the music that he leapt almost four metres from the choir loft above the stage. Cartwright recalls witnessing the accident from the middle of the main floor of the auditorium and rushing backstage to check on the patron. "An ambulance was called," she said, "but the young man was still smiling, and he didn't seem to have any

serious injuries." The patron was carried away on a stretcher and the performance went on with the ecstatic music continuing, although ushers were decidedly more watchful of audience members' proximity to balcony railings.

Co-presenting with other cultural groups grew and expanded over the years to become a cornerstone of the hall's programming mandate under current director of programming Jesse Kumagai, so that every new season could more closely mirror the mix of people and cultures that make up Toronto. Kumagai doesn't just peruse the lists of available acts that every agent sends around to concert presenters, he travels out to community events throughout the Greater Toronto Area to make sure that his programming reflects the tastes and needs of one of the most culturally diverse metropolitan areas in the world.

In September of 2008, just a month after his performance as part of the opening ceremonies for the Beijing Olympics was seen by more than one billion people across the globe, Chinese piano phenomenon Lang Lang arrived in Toronto for a week-long residency that included two performances with the Toronto Symphony Orchestra and a solo recital at Roy Thomson Hall. The week also included a live interview with Peter Oundjian at the Royal Ontario Museum and a master class at the Chinese Cultural Centre of Greater Toronto. The residency was a collaboration between the orchestra and the hall, and would serve as a model for future collaborative programming and artist residencies.

When the JUNO Awards returned to Toronto for its fortieth anniversary in 2011, the nation's musicians were celebrated in clubs and concert halls, on outdoor

Tony Bennett performs at Roy Thomson Hall, 2013.

Photo by Igor Vidyashev/ rockxposure.com.

stages, and in exhibits throughout the city. On the evening of March 22, Canadian classical musicians assembled at Roy Thomson Hall for a once-in-a-lifetime concert featuring four decades of JUNO Award winners and nominees. Hosted by Peter Oundjian, the concert featured performances by Winona Zelenka, Tafelmusik Baroque Orchestra, Duo Concertante, Gryphon Trio, Lara St. John, Anton Kuerti, Angèle Dubeau & La Pietà, Amici Chamber Ensemble, and the inimitable Measha Brueggergosman. It was one of the rare occasions when members of Canada's classical music community gathered to celebrate their own in a program that reflected the talent and diversity of the country's finest classical musicians.

Arthur Erickson's auditorium design makes the hall especially well suited to the spoken word, and Roy Thomson Hall has hosted numerous speakers as well as entertainers. The first big-name author to grace the stage solo was Deepak Chopra, finding a ready repeat audience from among his thousands of local readers in the late 1980s. The success of his visits helped lay the foundation for the venue's most lasting partnership for non-musical events: the Unique Lives & Experiences lecture series, currently produced by Howard Szigeti. Charles Cutts saw this series as a creative, easy-to-stage way to take advantage of the dark hall left behind after Toronto Symphony Orchestra daytime rehearsals on Mondays. Since 1993, almost one hundred distinguished women — including Margaret Thatcher, Maya Angelou, Julie Andrews, and Lily Tomlin — have visited the hall as part of this series that is part learning and part storytelling. Guests are invited to arrive early and dine tapas-style or enjoy a glass of wine before listening to the evening's speaker, and a short question-and-answer session following the lecture encourages guests to share their own experiences with their fellow attendees. Like Roy Thomson Hall's world music programming, Unique Lives & Experiences caters to people who might not otherwise attend other performances at the hall, further helping to fulfill the corporate mandate of bringing the best events to the greatest number of people possible.

In 2010, the hall became home to another high-profile speaker series, the Munk Debates, which offers a platform for influential thinkers and public figures to go head-to-head on major social and political issues facing Canada and the world. The first debate held at the hall featured former British prime minister Tony Blair facing author and essayist Christopher Hitchens on the question of religion's relative good to humankind. The event was widely covered in the media, and every seat in the house was filled by those eager to see the men Paul Harris of the *Guardian* newspaper called "the most famous recent Roman Catholic convert … and the charismatic but cancer-stricken skeptic" trade barbs. Hitchens easily had the better of Blair, but the audience seemed more interested in the topic at hand than who won or lost. Although the two subsequent debates the following year didn't capture the same international level of media attention, the events continue to be hugely popular, with tickets to the 2012 debate on the state of the European Union selling out in less than forty-eight hours.

The most recent spoken programming to launch at Roy Thomson Hall is National Geographic Live, a critically acclaimed series of lectures featuring scientists, explorers, and photographers sharing tales of their adventures in some of the most exotic locations around the world. Andy van Duym, who directs the series for National Geographic, says that these events strive to move the audience away from the digital world and help them reconnect with the "fundamental interest we have in storytelling" and the natural world. The first season's topics were diverse, ranging from underwater photography to the human genome; the latter event had the distinction of being the first in the hall's history to invite patrons to "send in a cheek swab and find out how your genetic history fits into the broader picture of humanity." The series was an unqualified success for both Roy Thomson Hall and National Geographic. This allowed organizers of the 2012–13 season to add a second night to each lecture in the four-lecture series, as well as a matinee series for school children.

Programming is an ever-evolving process that is as much about communities as it is about marketing. "When you're trying to develop new audiences and new relations with those communities, it's a lot of work and a lot of outreach," says Kumagai of his shifting objectives. "It's a slow but very rewarding process."

National Geographic Live, photojournalist Catherine Karnow talks about her photographs of Vietnam, 2013.

Photo by Jag Gundu.

CHAPTER 10

A Permanent Sense of Occasion

T HE STRIKING, ROUND modernity of Roy Thomson Hall signals to passersby that there is something not to be overlooked at the corner of King and Simcoe Streets. This ever-present sense of occasion promised by the exterior is echoed inside by spacious lobby areas that form a continuous loop around the auditorium. This encourages the sort of mixing and mingling that feeds the buzz of great social and musical events. Once guests pass the double doors into the hall itself, its circularity wraps the audience into a surprisingly close relationship with whatever is happening onstage. It's a combination of attributes that has made Arthur Erickson's structure so adaptable to all sorts of special events.

Thanks to a clutch of great talent, careful preparation, an electric concert, a national radio broadcast, and the subsequent release of a commemorative CD that continues to be a bestseller for CBC Records more than a dozen years later, the "Millennium Opera Gala," held at Roy Thomson Hall on the evening of December 31, 1999, was a signal event in the venue's first three decades.

The dawning of a new millennium represented a milestone deserving of a special musical commemoration, and

Facing page:
The 2007 gala.

Photo by Richard Beland.

Millennium Opera Gala CD, produced by CBC Records.

three years prior to that date, programmer Wende Cartwright had a notion to produce something "truly spectacular." A long-time opera fan, Cartwright was reminded every day of how many great Canadian singers, many with Toronto connections, were working and living abroad because of a lack of paid opportunities at home. Cartwright was already booking the world's finest for the hall's all-classical International Vocal Recitals series concerts but, for this occasion, she wanted a bred-in-Canada lineup for an event that would be as glamorous and memorable as the finest galas seen on any of the world's most prestigious stages.

The result of two years of figuring out logistics, negotiating with managers, and making nearly two dozen revisions to the final program, with CBC Radio producer Neil Crory and the corporation's programming committee, was an evening featuring sixteen singers, ranging from veteran international star tenor Ben Heppner to newcomer sopranos Isabel Bayrakdarian and Measha Brueggergosman. The youngest performer was eighteen-year-old bass Robert Pomakov, who had only just graduated from St. Michael's Choir School. Crory and Cartwright shared a passion

Ben Heppner, at the 25th Anniversary Gala, with La Scala Philharmonic, 2007.

Photo by Richard Beland.

for opera. With Crory's connoisseur tastes and insightful knowledge of young sing-ers and what they could do (often with a better understanding than they had), it made him an invaluable resource for programming a historic evening. Cartwright coordinated all the other details, from theatrical lighting to choice of gowns and hair styling. Christmas week for all the artists and organizers was spent in rehearsal.

The singers would perform solo arias as well as ensemble pieces from favourite operas, with a full orchestra largely made up of members of the Toronto Symphony Orchestra. The conductors were Mario Bernardi, who had made himself a fine reputation with Ottawa's National Arts Centre and the now-defunct CBC Radio orchestras, and Canadian Opera Company general director Richard Bradshaw.

The evening began early on New Year's Eve, at 7:30 p.m., to allay fears that the concert would be interrupted by computerized systems failing at midnight — a paranoia stoked by the Y2K bug. The bulk of tickets were gone the first week they went on sale — all of them to individuals, rather than a more common mix of corporate and private seats. And when the CBC announced that budget cuts had put the commemorative album release in jeopardy, a last-minute fundrais-ing campaign by the hall's development team found the needed money in a few weeks, helping preserve the event for posterity.

This was the single most expensive concert that the Corporation of Massey Hall and Roy Thomson Hall had ever produced, largely due to the large cast of soloists and the extensive rehearsal period. Even so, it nearly broke even, coming in only $4,000 in the red. Audience buzz and reviews were unanimously posi-tive. Urjo Kareda prophetically wrote in the *Globe and Mail* that "It felt like the beginning of an era." That is exactly what it turned out to be and, without a doubt, helped Bradshaw and the Canadian Opera Company establish the momentum needed in a final push to build its own home, a dream realized six years later with the opening of the Four Seasons Centre for the Performing Arts just a few blocks away from Roy Thomson Hall. The afterglow from the "Millennium Opera Gala" lasted for years, encouraging the founders of the Luminato festival to request a similar event for the first opening week in 2007. That concert, the "Luna Gala," also brought together many of this country's finest operatic talents.

Several other gala concerts loom large in audiences' collective memories. One of them was a landmark in the history of the Toronto Symphony Orchestra. Known as the "Great Gathering," the March 1987 bash feted the retirement of Walter Homburger, who had led a double life as the city's top musical impresario since the late 1940s while working as the orchestra's managing director for a quar-ter century. The concert, which didn't end until well after midnight, was broadcast live across the country by CBC Television. Some of the biggest stars of the classi-cal music world gathered alongside symphony players on stage in a program that included orchestral and choral chestnuts as well as chamber music.

Walter Homburger at the
Great Gathering, 1987.

Photo by Brian Pickell.
Courtesy of the Toronto Archives.

In *Begins with the Oboe*, his history of the Toronto Symphony Orchestra, archivist Richard Warren writes, "The final work on the program was the overture to Johann Strauss's opera *Die Fledermaus*, with Isaac Stern as concertmaster, Yo-Yo Ma as principal cello, Pinchas Zukerman as principal viola, Jean-Pierre Rampal as principal flute, and a percussion section augmented with Maureen Forrester, Seiji Ozawa, Mstislav Rostropovich, Victor Feldbrill, and Elmer Iseler." All of these great artists performed for free, as long as their travel and accommodation expenses were covered. This allowed the orchestra to raise $1.15 million towards its endowment fund. Young musicians from across Ontario were in the audience. Even the *New York Times* saw fit to recognize the landmark event in a pre-concert feature.

Two years later, the Toronto Symphony Orchestra created more gala buzz by offering a joint concert with the Israel Philharmonic Orchestra, billed as "A Fusion of Harmonies." The Roy Thomson Hall stage had to be extended out into the auditorium to accommodate 230 musicians playing as one under star conductor Zubin Mehta. The TSO's Günther Herbig also conducted.

Queen Elizabeth II and Prince Phillip have visited the hall twice as part of royal tours. The first was in October 1984, to mark the 150th anniversary of the founding of the Town of York. The second, eighteen years later, was in 2002, when Roy Thomson Hall became the backdrop for Canada's commemoration of the Queen's Golden Jubilee. The CBC produced the first concert, which was an hour long, as a variety show presenting Toronto's finest classical, jazz, and pop musicians, with the Toronto Symphony Orchestra and music director Andrew Davis acting as all-purpose accompanists. Produced by the Department of Canadian Heritage and the National Arts Centre, the 2002 royal gala was also a large-scale talent show, but with a national scope. With actor Colm Feore as master of ceremonies, the Queen, a full house of dignitaries, regular patrons, and thousands of viewers on CBC Television saw a parade of talent that included the Newfoundland Symphony Youth Choir, Quebec pop singer Ginette Reno, National Ballet of Canada and Royal Winnipeg

Queen Elizabeth II was welcomed by Prime Minister Brian Mulroney in 1984. In 2002, she was escorted by Prime Minister Jean Chrétien and shook hands with the artists on stage, including Oscar Peterson.

Top right: Courtesy of Gary Beechey/BDS Studios.
Bottom: Courtesy of the National Arts Centre.

Ray Charles on stage
at Roy Thomson Hall,
at the 2000 gala.

Photo © *National Post/*
Glenn Lowson.

Ballet principal dancers Rex Harrington and Evelyn Hart (Hart had also danced, opposite Frank Augustyn, for the Queen eight years earlier), opera singers Measha Brueggergosman and Michael Schade, the Tragically Hip, the Oscar Peterson Quartet, and the acrobats of Cirque du Soleil. Cutts recalls the thrill of being able to greet Her Majesty and Prince Philip — and of saving the regal couple potential embarrassment by catching the Royal Consort after he nearly tripped on an audio-visual cable.

Other highlights among galas that have lit up Erickson's circular auditorium include "A Night in Old Vienna," an April 1994 celebration of the eighty-fifth birthday of musician, impresario, and big dreamer Nicholas Goldschmidt. This individual likely had a hand in more special classical concerts at Roy Thomson Hall than anyone else. Goldschmidt's final and grandest gala of all, "The Joy of Niki," was pulled together after his death in 2004 at age ninety-five. The Nicholas Goldschmidt tribute committee was chaired by past board chair Suzanne Bradshaw, with CBC producer Robert Cooper serving as artistic director. Nine of Toronto's finest singers; seven choirs; members of the Toronto Symphony Orchestra, Canadian Opera Company Orchestra, and National Ballet Orchestra; and conductors Helmuth Rilling and Mario Bernardi spent two hours celebrating the entrepreneur's legacy in words and music. "No single concert can adequately sum up the extraordinary contributions that Nicholas Goldschmidt made to Canada's musical life over more than a half-century, or the colourful musical kaleidoscope that was his life," wrote Cooper in the evening's program. Cooper described Goldschmidt as a musical pioneer: "He founded festivals, travelled the world to seek out new and different musical idioms to bring back to Canadian audiences, and consistently championed the creation and performance of new repertoire by our own composers." People from the capacity audience that day agreed that this musical memorial had done a great man justice, walking out not crying, but smiling.

The Corporation of Massey Hall and Roy Thomson Hall has used its flagship stage to produce seventeen of its own fundraising galas since its glass-and-chrome doors opened in 1982. Reflecting the varied tastes of its patrons, the invited stars have spanned the classical, jazz, blues, world music, and popular genres. The marquee attraction at the first Roy Thomson Hall Gala was the Berlin Philharmonic

Left: Tom MacMillan, chair of the Board of Governors 2005–08.

Right: Eileen Costello and Richard Hamm, gala co-chairs for 2009 (Pink Martini), 2010 (Mariinsky Orchestra), 2011 (Vienna Philharmonic Orchestra), and 2012 (Lyle Lovett).

Photos by Richard Beland.

Orchestra, considered by many symphony lovers one of the top three orchestras in the world, led by its principal conductor at the time, Claudio Abbado. Two seasons later, it was the Boston Symphony's turn to make music, led by music director Seiji Ozawa, who had cut his North American conducting teeth with the Toronto Symphony Orchestra in the mid-1960s. Great divas to grace these special events have included Cecilia Bartoli and Denyce Graves. Popular entertainers with equally impressive pedigrees have included Tom Jones, Ray Charles, B.B. King, Cesaria Evora, and k.d. Lang. The legendary Tony Bennett ushered in the twenty-first century with a gala concert on January 17, 2000 — and Pink Martini is scheduled to celebrate Roy Thomson Hall's thirtieth anniversary season with their cosmopolitan flair. As Cutts explains it, the organization has proved over and over its commitment to "promising a lot and delivering more."

Besides being home to glittering events for both landlord and permanent tenants, Roy Thomson Hall has also enjoyed a thriving career as a gala venue-for-hire, hosting fundraising concerts and performances to benefit not-for-profit organizations. In an average year, six to eight such occasions are booked into the building — usually in the fall, when the calendar already bulges with gala screenings for the Toronto International Film Festival, followed by the start of the regular Toronto Symphony Orchestra concert season.

Over the years, benefit galas have raised money for medical research, hospital foundations, environmental causes, and the fight against poverty and homelessness. Recent performances of Beatles music by Classic Albums Live have raised funds for the Cornerstone 52 Foundation. This was preceded by a calypso-themed benefit for sickle cell anemia research and special events to raise money and awareness for Canada's Walk of Fame, whose stars grace the Simcoe Street sidewalk outside the building's main entrance. Oscar Peterson and his quartet jazzed up "Hazel's Concert of Hope" in 2005. Comedian Jerry Seinfeld stood up solo on stage for the Mount Sinai Hospital Foundation. Great Canadian musicians and composers gathered for a special evening marking the fortieth anniversary of the Juno Awards, and SOCAN held its presentation night there for the first time in 2011. And, when it opened its new building on Wellington Street in 2011, the Ritz-Carlton hotel organized a dinner on the stage of Roy Thomson Hall to benefit community outreach nutrition programs offered by neighbouring St. Andrew's Church, on King Street.

Sachertorte, flown in from the Hotel Sacher in Vienna for guests at the 2011 Vienna Philharmonic Gala.

Photo by Tom Sandler.

Thirty years in, the hall looks poised to keep its prime status as a downtown destination for special events. When annual charity events grow past a certain size, they strain the seating and stage capacities of hotel ballrooms, so organizers turn to Roy Thomson Hall to accommodate their special occasions. Although there is a catering kitchen situated in the building's lower floor, galas require the building to rent additional warming ovens, which are strategically placed under stairways so that patrons can be guaranteed hot food at mealtime. Although this is a big venue that hosts big names, success is always in the details.

So much of this book has outlined what goes on inside the walls at Roy Thomson Hall, but there is something special outside, as well. Canada's Walk of Fame greets anyone walking along King Street West and Simcoe Street, linking the hall with the Royal Alexandra and Princess of Wales Theatres across the street with dozens of stars embedded in the pavement, all speaking to the constellation of remarkable talents that this country has produced. And as the hall welcomes each new generation of artists and fans, the Walk of Fame grows as well.

Jim Carrey celebrating his star on the Canadian Walk of Fame in 2004, in front of Roy Thomson Hall on Simcoe Street.

Courtesy of Rick Bell.

The hall at night, when most patrons see it.

Photo by Richard Beland.

CHAPTER 11

From Concert Hall to Modern Movie Palace

ALTHOUGH THE GOVERNORS of Massey Hall intended their new building to serve many purposes in the community, they probably never imagined that one of the many fancy hats it would wear would be that of a movie palace. As it turned out, Arthur Erickson's edifice has been just as welcoming to screen actors — the likes of Lauren Bacall, Al Pacino, Shirley MacLaine, George Clooney, Catherine Deneuve, and Bollywood royal Shah Rukh Khan, among so many others — as it is to musicians, thanks to its starring role as the gala venue of the Toronto International Film Festival for the last two decades.

It is a role that has continued to grow as the epicentre of the annual festival — now considered among the world's most prestigious locations for the premiere of new films — shifted from Yorkville to the western downtown core with the opening of the TIFF Bell Lightbox festival headquarters at the corner of King and John Streets in September 2010.

The Toronto International Film Festival was founded in 1976 as the Festival of Festivals. Its inaugural edition, attended by thirty-five thousand movie buffs, screened 127 films from thirty countries. Films were shown at the Uptown Cinema on Yonge Street, neighbouring theatres in the Hudson's Bay and Manulife Centres, and the Cumberland Cinemas in Yorkville. The festival's premier venue was the University Theatre on Bloor Street West, right across from St. Thomas Street.

The elegantly curved modern facade of the University Theatre (now the entrance to a Pottery Barn) immediately became associated with the growing list of filmmakers and celebrities arriving in Toronto after Labour Day for landmark

Facing page: A crowd gathers outside the main doors to take their seats for a TIFF screening in 2006.

Photo by Richard Beland.

premieres. It helped burnish the reputation of the city's so-called Mink Mile, a stretch of Bloor Street anchored around the Holt Renfrew department store and its posh train of high-end merchants. The proximity of the Four Seasons Hotel and dozens of bars, restaurants, galleries, and boutiques in nearby Yorkville stirred together convenience and glamour for thousands of international guests.

The early years of the Festival of Festivals also coincided with the rise of multiplexing, when the big, original movie houses were shuttered or gutted in order to accommodate multiple screening rooms, some not much larger than a comfortable home rec room. In 1981, the Famous Players movie chain, owner of the University Theatre, announced plans to close the building so that the valuable real estate could be put to other uses. Toronto mayor Art Eggleton and a number of other influential voices spoke out against the move and the effects it might have on Bloor Street, as well as the film festival, but Famous Players persevered and succeeded in closing the theatre five years later, following the conclusion of the 1986 Festival of Festivals. All of the original festival venues, save for the Varsity cinemas in the Manulife Centre, have also since vanished into the history books.

Having lost its home for gala presentations, organizers turned to the theatre at Ryerson Polytechnic Institute (now Ryerson University) on Gerrard Street East, which holds slightly more than 1,200 people. "But it didn't quite have the sense of occasion we were looking for," says current Toronto International Film Festival director and CEO Piers Handling of the 1950s facility, built for function rather than looks. The design of the main Ryerson campus and the narrowness of Gerrard Street don't lend themselves easily to red-carpet arrivals, although the festival has continued to use the theatre as a regular screening venue, thanks to its generous size.

Scouring the city for auditoriums with more pizzazz, the festival decided to enlist the Elgin Theatre, a gilded auditorium originally built as a vaudeville theatre on Yonge Street across from the Eaton Centre, as its gala destination for two years. And, like the Ryerson Theatre, it continues to serve the festival to this day. According to Handling, the gala screenings quickly outgrew the Elgin's 1,400-seat capacity,

Bruce Springsteen and his wife, Patti Scialfa, greet fans outside the hall on their way to the screening of *The Promise: The Making of Darkness on the Edge of Town*, 2010.

Photo by Richard Beland.

U2's Bono and The Edge on the Roy Thomson Hall stage at the premiere of the film *From the Sky Down* at TIFF 2011.

Photo by Jag Gundu.

forcing the festival to hunt again for a larger venue, preferably with two thousand or more seats. Handling admits that organizers were also hoping to find something with more imposing curb appeal. The Elgin, as meticulously restored and ornate as it is on the inside, sits anonymously on Victoria Street, extending a relatively modest, narrow main entrance to Yonge Street. Rather than celebrating a patron's arrival, it serves as a long conduit that quickly gets congested, sapping the thrill of spotting celebrity stilettos on the ever-present red carpet. The festival director tells

Kate Beckinsale being led through the hall at the 2008 TIFF screening of *Nothing but the Truth*.

Photo by Richard Beland.

of a gala screening in the late 1980s that featured comedian and actor Billy Crystal as one of the guests of honour. When Crystal's cab came to a halt at the Yonge Street curb, the actor looked out the window and said, "Is this it?" Handling recalls.

In 1987, Toronto businessman and impresario Garth Drabinsky, then head of Cineplex Entertainment, insisted on a big closing-night gala screening for Paul Newman's remake of *The Glass Menagerie*, which starred John Malkovich and Newman's wife Joanne Woodward. Handling explains that Drabinsky, who had money invested in this release, made sure the stars would show up, and wanted to hold the event at Roy Thomson Hall. The experience was such a success that Drabinsky asked for a repeat the following year, when Shirley MacLaine graced the Simcoe Street sidewalk for the debut of her acclaimed turn as an eccentric piano teacher in *Madame Sousatzka*.

Handling liked Roy Thomson Hall's natural street presence as a standalone building, further enhanced by its striking design. Here was a venue that could more than compete with the Palais des Festivals et des Congrès in Cannes, which opened its doors in 1982, the same year as Toronto's landmark. "It had a place where you could pull the limos up. It was a place that could help create buzz and excitement, which we really needed," Handling recalls.

The festival CEO says organizers still needed to get the attention of Hollywood, even in the late 1980s. Roy Thomson Hall helped them achieve this goal, with a team of experts who descended on the place over the summer months to change it into an oversized cinema. "Our tech team did a spectacular job, dressing the hall and turning it into a movie house," he remembers. The makeover included bringing in sound engineers from Dolby Laboratories to ensure that film buffs would get the right surround-sound experience to go along with the giant screen that hung down in front of the organ.

The building's status as a perennial festival venue was still a few years off, though. "With our modest budget in those days, we couldn't quite conceive of four-walling Roy Thomson Hall, of turning it into a cinema, of doing the kind of technical make-over that you actually have to do," says Handling, "so it took us another ten years before we got into the financial position where we felt we could take that gamble."

When the festival did take the plunge, then renamed the Toronto International Film Festival, it discovered that its prestige marquee was a sure thing, not a gamble at all. After a period of negotiation between Charles Cutts and TSO managing director Max Tapper that included a demand for reduced rent, the Toronto Symphony Orchestra moved back its annual season-opening concerts by a week in order to accommodate the festival. Since no self-respecting movie house is complete without bags of fragrant, hot popcorn, Roy Thomson Hall rented a popcorn machine for festival screenings in the early years. Once staff overcame their misgivings about butter stains on the carpeting, everyone realized that the snack was as popular among gala audiences as at a suburban multiplex. It also didn't take long to discover how profitable peddling bags of popcorn can be, enticing the hall to invest in its own permanent popcorn maker, affectionately known by building staff and managers as Big Bertha. As

During the ten days of TIFF, the venue sells more than 10,000 bags of popcorn.

Photo by Richard Beland.

with so many other investments that could be seen as single-purpose expenses, Big Bertha has proven to be popular at family-oriented events at the venue, including a 2011 screening of *The Wizard of Oz* presented by the Toronto Symphony Orchestra.

It's the attention to detail that has solidified the relationship between TIFF and Roy Thomson Hall. "A number of filmmakers who have come through for world premieres have said that this is the best projection they have seen of their film, ever," boasts Handling of the top-level equipment used for gala screenings. "Heads of studios like Sony, Warner Brothers and Paramount are exacting about everything being perfect," he adds.

He points out that the building's expansive lobby spaces and suites of rooms on the stage level have proven to be a boon for anyone wanting to have a party or dinner on the premises during the festival. "Sponsors have learned to use the hall over the years," Handling says. Every year, the list of ancillary events has increased to the point where the closing party is now held at the venue, rather than at Harbourfront Centre or the Liberty Grand complex on the CNE grounds, which were the locations of closing parties in the more distant past. Now, Handling says, people come out of the film and "don't have to go out for a hike."

The 2002 acoustical renovation integrated many of TIFF's technical needs, such as wiring and baffles for a variety of additional sound system requirements, into walls and bulkheads. The enhancements also made the orchestra level easier to navigate by people who, Handling says, prefer to stand and chat until the lights go down for the start of a screening. The original seating configuration, which had no aisles down the middle of the auditorium, made it difficult for people to get in and out of their seats quickly. The wood added to the floors and walls during the renovation also warmed up the all-grey interior. "The hall is big but, when it's full, there is an intimacy there," says Handling.

Even so, Handling says that he and his colleagues have learned to promote Roy Thomson Hall for the festival's biggest events only. He admits that many filmmakers have an attraction to traditional movie theatres and spaces. Also, he adds, "A lot of films that come to the festival don't want to overplay their hand."

Natalie Portman signs autographs outside Roy Thomson Hall at TIFF 2009 on her way to the gala screening of her movie *Love and Other Impossible Pursuits*.

Photo by George Pimentel, WireImage / Getty for TIFF.

So they want to limit the number of seats at a screening, at which point something like the Elgin Theatre works better. Other filmmakers are superstitious, wanting to clutch a lucky rabbit's foot from a previous triumph. Handling cites the example of filmmaker Jason Reitman, whose acclaimed 2009 movie *Up in the Air* received six Academy Award nominations. That film had its Toronto International Film Festival premiere at the Ryerson Theatre, and, despite the fact that Reitman's name and reputation are now enough to fill Roy Thomson Hall, the director won't consider having one of his movies shown anywhere else during the festival.

Handling believes many film industry players view King and Simcoe as the destination for older, more conservative and corporate movie events, largely because the building is now associated with big sponsor parties, as well. "They feel younger, hipper audiences go elsewhere in the festival," he says.

That may be the inside story, but there's also a very public outside story to Roy Thomson Hall's relationship with the city and the film festival. Handling admits that he and many other seasoned festival patrons miss the immediacy and excitement of seeing limousine after limousine pull up to the main entrance at Roy Thomson Hall on Simcoe Street. Until the roadway was extended south of the rail lands, linking it to the lakeshore, the City of Toronto allowed film festival organizers to cordon off two of its three lanes of traffic for gala events. Stars would slip out of a lineup as much as thirty limousines long and walk the red carpet through the glass doors, within an arm's reach of the people who were waiting in and around the lobby to see the movie. Handling fondly recalls the thrill of seeing hundreds of people peering over lobby railings and balconies to get a glimpse of their favourite stars. The arrival that created the biggest fuss one year was Jackie Chan's, when people in the crowd would not stop screaming. "Just the noise level was amazing," Handling remembers.

When the city was no longer willing to curtail regular traffic on Simcoe Street in 2008, the festival moved the VIP entrance over to David Pecaut Square, the park that separates Roy Thomson Hall from the Metro Hall complex to its west. The big difference, says Handling,

TIFF reception in the North Court.

Photo by Richard Beland.

View of the hall from
David Pecaut Square.

Photo by Richard Beland.

View of the red carpet
setup from the entrance
into Roy Thomson Hall at
a TIFF screening.

Photo by Richard Beland.

is that the hundreds, sometimes thousands, of gawkers who crowd the square "are
not actually the people who are going to come see the movie."

In recent years, the Toronto International Film Festival has added family
screenings on weekends, bringing parents and children to a sometimes unfamil-
iar part of downtown Toronto. The same has happened with the Greater Toronto
Area's massive South Asian community since Bollywood premieres have found a
place on the festival's gala roster.

Handling says he and festival staff were initially unprepared for the level of
frenzy among Bollywood fans. At the first gala screening of a Bollywood movie a
few years ago, members of the audience rushed the Roy Thomson Hall stage, and
every available member of the festival's staff had to be mobilized instantly to make
sure no one would try to climb up onto it. It's just one of dozens of special memories the festival director has of his prime venue. Another incident that turned
into a festival legend occurred when director Paul Schrader and his star, Lauren
Bacall, were present. The presentation of their film broke down just ten minutes
into the screening. "It's a nightmare for us, the organizers," Handling remembers,
"but what the audience remembers at the end of the day is Paul Schrader and Lauren Bacall doing a song-and-dance number on stage to keep them entertained."

History continues to be written, as the festival now screens about 350 movies
every year, with attendance that has surpassed a half-million people. Roy Thomson
Hall, which hosts twenty galas over ten days every September, "used to feel so
detached from the festival," Handling says. But now, with the new Ritz-Carlton

hotel open a few metres away on Wellington Street, the move of the red carpet to David Pecaut Square, and TIFF headquarters just a block away, Handling says, "we reconstructed festival mass downtown."

The big movie buzz in town may belong to the Toronto International Film Festival, but the hall has proven its flexibility in a number of other presentations that have given film pride of place. A classic of the moviemaking art had its Canadian premiere with full orchestral accompaniment in 1987 at the venue. Sergei Eisenstein's 1938 epic *Alexander Nevsky* featured the full Toronto Symphony Orchestra and the Toronto Mendelssohn Choir performing Sergei Prokofiev's score, with actor Donald Sutherland acting as master of ceremonies. This gala film presentation was in support of the Canadian Centre for Advanced Film Studies. In the fall of 1995, Roy Thomson Hall presented the Canadian premiere of Philip Glass's *La Belle et la Bête*, a work that combined film, concert, and opera. It was so well received that Glass and his collaborators returned to the venue in the spring of 1999 to conclude the North American tour of *Monsters of Grace*, another supersized multimedia experiment that may have marked the first time anyone at Roy Thomson Hall had been asked to put on a pair of 3-D glasses for a concert.

The *National Post*'s quote from Glass, who described the future of opera at the time of *Monsters of Grace,* could just as well have applied to the venue in which it was being presented: "One thing is for sure. What I call the four elements of music theatre — image, text, music and movement — are being redefined in terms of each other in very new ways. That, I'm sure, will go on into the future."

CHAPTER 12

Meeting, Celebration, Business, and Worship

ROY THOMSON HALL proved its versatility as a movie house with patrons of the Toronto International Film Festival. It has also, since early days, served many other functions, including as a substitute convention centre, community hall, and place of worship. Ultimately, this is much more than a place to see live performances — it is, and always has been, a multi-purpose facility.

During initial fundraising for New Massey Hall, the board of governors had committed to running the place without governmental or corporate operating subsidies, and renting space for a variety of business and cultural activities has gone a long way to helping keep that promise. A building the size of Roy Thomson Hall is costly to operate when there is nothing going on. According to former board of governors chair Suzanne Bradshaw, renting space not only pays bills but also serves as a form of community outreach. "I know there are some people who feel a concert hall is a concert hall, and nothing else," she says, "but as far as I'm concerned, anything that brings people into Roy Thomson Hall is important."

Just about every type of event imaginable has attracted crowds to the building over the past thirty years. Jugglers and trampoline artists added circus flair to the gala birthday celebration for former governor general Roland Michener in 1985. Hundreds of young partyers danced to trance music at a rave in 2001. The building has even starred in a Hollywood blockbuster or two; pay close attention to the *X-Men* (2000) and *Total Recall* (2012) films, and you will notice the hall standing in for a futuristic or high-tech locale. Staff boasts that there's hardly any event or unusual need they haven't found some way to accommodate.

Roy Thomson Hall even acted as a focal point for international politics at the Toronto Economic Summit of June 1988. Security and the need to follow strict protocol were tight as the leaders of the G7 industrialized nations met in Ontario's capital. Ronald Reagan, president of the United States, arrived at Roy Thomson Hall by helicopter from Queen's Park, just a few blocks up University Avenue. The other leaders — Canadian prime minister Brian Mulroney, French president François Mitterrand, West Germany's chancellor Helmut Kohl, Italy's prime minister Ciriaco de Mita, Japan's prime minister Noboru Takeshita, United Kingdom's prime minister Margaret Thatcher, and the president of the European Commission, Jacques Delors — chose more conventional arrivals. Members of the board of governors, including Edward Pickering and John Lawson, were among local dignitaries chosen to greet each arriving head of state, adding more than a little bit of lustre to their years of volunteer work with the organization.

When the hall opened in 1982, it wasn't the intention of management to promote the venue as an all-purpose rental location. The buzz surrounding Toronto's new landmark did the advertising itself. "People were interested in the exciting new kid on the block, and the demand was overwhelming," according to Roy Thomson Hall's Lillian Thalheimer. Because the building's staff has made a point of accommodating a wide range of special event requirements, the building has generated a significant amount of return business. Janice McKenzie Hadfield, who initially handled venue rentals, understood the business of nurturing relationships with clients. "She was masterful at it," says Thalheimer. "Janice anticipated the interest from existing Massey Hall clients in the new location. She built on these relationships while establishing new ones. Many long-standing Massey Hall clients, such as the Salvation Army, St. Michael's Choir School and the Toronto District School Board, remain part of the rental family at both halls to this day."

Originally hired as a weekend receptionist to field phones that were ringing off the hook with rental inquiries, Thalheimer is one of the hall's longest-serving

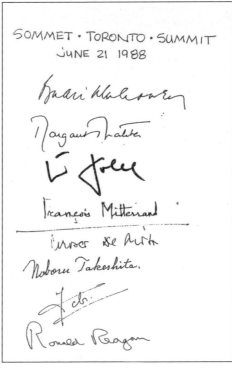

SOMMET · TORONTO · SUMMIT
JUNE 21 1988

Brian Mulroney

Margaret Thatcher

[Helmut Kohl]

François Mitterrand

Ciriaco de Mita

Noboru Takeshita.

[Jacques Delors]

Ronald Reagan

Left: Camera crews and the press take their seats in the auditorium as the G7 leaders meet to take questions on stage during the Economic Summit in 1988.

Photo by Paul J. Hoeffler.

Right: On June 21, 1988, the heads of state and the heads of government signed the Roy Thomson Hall guest book: Brian Mulroney, Margaret Thatcher, Helmut Kohl, François Mitterrand, Ciriaco de Mita, Noboru Takeshita, Jacques Delors, and Ronald Reagan.

employees, having done everything from bartend to replace buttons on original general manager William Armstrong's suit jacket. Today she is associate director of bookings and event services, responsible not only for rentals, but also for the entire Massey Hall and Roy Thomson Hall calendars.

"The challenge that we have for all events is to find pockets of opportunity when the stage is quiet," says venue sales manager Robin Howarth. During the Toronto Symphony Orchestra season, rehearsals are often booked in the morning or afternoon on non-performance days, making Howarth's job of scheduling events something of a creative endeavour. "My job, and that of Krista Beaudry, the bookings associate, is to coordinate times and spaces so there's no overlap, and guide clients and advise them." A wide range of spaces encircling the auditorium makes accommodating multiple events on the same day a bit easier. And on any night, a catered dinner for several hundred people could be being served in the south lobby of the hall; the courtyard patio or American Express Lounge might be set up for a smaller, more intimate reception; while in the Pickering or Green Room, building operations staff can be preparing for a corporate meeting to be held the following morning. At peak booking capacity, which is usually reached during events like the Toronto International Film Festival, the hall can accommodate as many as six events at once. Often, the setup for an upcoming event is getting underway as a previous event is finishing. Howarth compares organizing setups and takedowns to "jigsaw puzzles, where you have to lay the events

Backstage sound equipment for the live CBC-TV broadcast of the Golden Jubilee Gala, 2002.

The 2011 Vienna Philharmonic Gala.

Photo by Tom Sandler.

David Johnston, Governor General of Canada, and Charles Cutts at Queen Elizabeth II's Diamond Jubilee Medal Ceremony, at Roy Thomson Hall, 2012.

Photo by Doug Foulds.

Intermission at The Music Store.

Photo by Tom Sandler.

one after the other, and look at what equipment and staff each event needs, and how that might be shared."

Integral to most rentals is the hall's food and beverage staff, who work in conjunction with clients and caterers to ensure smells and tastes are as dazzling as the sights and sounds. Richard Kalitsis, who manages the food and beverage department at the hall, begins planning events as much as six months ahead of time. "Our team has done literally thousands of events," says Kalitsis, who adds that, "we don't have misses."

Track record notwithstanding, the manager does recall a near miss with a caterer from an outside company. The lobbies of the hall had been decorated with, among other things, bales of hay, and someone thought it would be a nice touch to place a gas burner atop one of the bales. "Needless to say," Kalitsis smiles, "dry grass and flame don't mix." A small fire broke out but was quickly doused by a member of the food and beverage staff. This led directly to a new building policy that specifies a fire extinguisher be present for every open flame indoors.

Running on petroleum but far less flammable than burners are the many vehicles that have graced the hall's stage and lobby areas. Patrons attending concerts have undoubtedly noticed the frequent presence of one car or another in the hall's vestibule, but might be surprised to learn that a Porsche Le Mans racer was once parked at the main entrance during a private event.

Lexus cars prominently displayed: being driven into the hall for a sponsored event, and in the North Court pond.

Left: Photo by Stephen McGrath.
Right: Photo by Richard Beland.

The venue has also been used as an automotive showroom on occasion, with Ford, Chrysler, BMW, Mercedes-Benz, and Lexus among the manufacturers who have taken advantage of the hall to launch new models for dealers and sales personnel. To move vehicles into and around the building, purpose-built ramps commissioned by the hall are laid atop the lobby stairs by building services staff, who also remove panes of glass in the entryway so that professional drivers can drive the cars into the building. Once in place, the battery terminals are disconnected, the gas tanks are locked, and the vehicles are cleaned and polished, ready for their own brand of show business. Pedestrians and drivers travelling along the south and east sides of the building are accustomed to seeing long-time car sponsor Lexus's latest models displayed in and outside the building. A committed venue sponsor alongside American Express and Rolex, Lexus and the hall share a similar "pursuit of perfection."

One of the more popular uses for Roy Thomson Hall has been as a venue for large corporate meetings. Companies including AIG, PricewaterhouseCoopers, Bell Canada, Sun Life, Magna International, Franklin Templeton Investments, Sherritt International, and Thomson Corporation have all held business meetings on stage or in the lobbies and meeting rooms. The success of these events is due to the attention paid to detail by all departments, making sure each client's needs are met and every event feels customized.

The size and scale of the auditorium make it tailor-made for all sorts of occasions that bring people together. Every Christmas Eve since 1989, Metropolitan Community Church of Toronto has held a festive service in the building. Embodying the true spirit of inclusiveness, the same space has served Christian worshippers as well as Muslims celebrating the birth of the prophet Muhammad. In a secular vein, OCAD University rents the auditorium and lobbies for its graduation exercises, and the Law Society of Upper Canada has been holding its Call to the Bar ceremonies at the hall for twenty-four years.

The hall has also been used for many award ceremonies. One of the most notable was on October 21, 1990, with "A Tribute to Edmund C. Bovey." It included fourteen of Canada's major arts organizations, which the CEO of Norcen Energy Resources had been involved with up to his death that year.

They put together a program under the artistic direction of Roy Thomson Hall's Muriel Sherrin. The hall was a fitting venue, as Ed Bovey was a driving force in the building of Roy Thomson Hall. The finale of the evening was the presentation of the new Edmund C. Bovey Award, "to honour a business professional who has demonstrated a lifetime of significant support or leadership in arts and culture in Canada." It was presented that night to Mrs. Peg Bovey, in honour of her husband.

The building has also been used for commemorations of a more solemn sort. On September 29, 2006, it became the backdrop for a celebration of the life of Kenneth Thomson — son of Roy Thomson, and a regular patron and proud benefactor of the hall. The family had organized a private funeral shortly after Thomson died on June 12 that year, but it was felt that some sort of public event was also in order. Anecdotes told by family and friends were interspersed with music in the hour-long memorial, which included music by the Toronto Symphony Orchestra, Rita MacNeil, and the Men of the Deeps. "If the definition and measure of a human being are the lives that are touched, he touched them in such a unique, genuine, and open manner," said eldest son David Thomson during a speech. The words rang true with long-time Roy Thomson Hall staff, who recall how the businessman and avid art collector would invariably remember the names of spouses and children, and would always ask how they were doing with genuine curiosity. In a reflection of Thomson's often very ordinary tastes and pleasures, the reception afterwards included a selection of his favourite sweets: M&Ms, black licorice, and Baskin-Robbins ice cream.

The commemoration of Ken Thomson's life opened the doors to other celebrations. In early 2008, the hall played host to a tribute concert honouring the life of Canadian jazz legend Oscar Peterson, organized with the assistance of the National Arts Centre in Ottawa. Peterson was the recipient of the 1987 Roy Thomson Hall Award, which recognizes creative, performing, administrative, volunteer, or philanthropic contributions to Toronto's musical life by a person, ensemble, or organization. He was also a long-time resident of the city, and the hall was a natural place to celebrate his life. Some fans lined up hours before dawn to guarantee their admission to the free event, which featured performances from, among others, Quincy Jones, Herbie Hancock, and Measha Brueggergosman. By the time the doors opened, the queue of people waiting to pay their respects began at the box office and wound along King Street and through David Pecaut Square. Lydia Burton, who was third in line that morning, told the *Toronto Star* that the event was a great "gift from Roy Thomson Hall," a sentiment that was shared by the hundreds of people who braved the January cold for a chance to say goodbye to Peterson and celebrate his life and legacy.

The public line up for the Oscar Peterson Memorial Concert, which was held at Roy Thomson Hall on January 12, 2008.

Top: *Toronto Star*/GetStock.com

Roy Thomson Hall was also the scene of a major public tribute in August of 2011, for the state funeral of federal NDP leader Jack Layton. Layton and his wife Olivia Chow had attended every Christmas Eve service organized there by Metropolitan Community Church. Having become leader of the official opposition

Thousands of people, many of them dressed in orange, pay tribute to former NDP leader Jack Layton as his funeral inside Roy Thomson Hall is simulcast into neighbouring David Pecaut Square, August 27, 2011.

Top: The Canadian Press / Michael Hudson
Bottom: The Canadian Press / Frank Gunn

only months before, and with deep roots in Toronto going back to his days as a local councillor, Layton was a much-loved political figure. Thousands of people who remembered him fondly converged at City Hall, where Layton's body lay in repose. Many used chalk to fill every inch of available space in Nathan Phillips Square with messages of love and support for the late politician and his family. That outpouring of sentiment followed the funeral procession through the downtown core to King and Simcoe Streets, where the farewell ceremony spilled out of the auditorium into David Pecaut Square.

Although it was a sad occasion, the mood at Roy Thomson Hall was positive, as Layton had hoped it would be. In the days before his death, he had requested that his funeral be a public celebration of life rather than a time of sombre remembrance. Outside the hall, a New Orleans–style funeral band spontaneously began playing before the service began. Inside, Lorraine Segato of the Parachute Club performed Layton's favourite pop song, the uplifting "Rise Up," at the end of the service. One of the largest events that the hall's staff had ever worked on was arranged in under a week in coordination with the Department of Canadian Heritage. While the details of the service were being planned, the food and beverage staff scrambled to find enough cans of Orange Crush for the more than 2,500 people who would attend the reception that was to follow the funeral. "It took a lot of effort," says Richard Kalitsis, but it was worth the work when guests toasted Layton's memory with the soda that had come to be identified with the New Democratic Party's achievements in the previous federal election.

When all is said and done, "we're in the business to support ourselves," says Lillian Thalheimer, and that's the case whether Roy Thomson Hall is acting as a presenter or a renter. Priority is given to the former, certainly, but Thalheimer maintains, "If it can be rented, we will rent it." She recalls having hired out both the roof and the boiler room as filming locations, and is content to just "go with it," within reason.

This means there are probably new, future uses for the building no one has even considered — yet.

CHAPTER 13

Connecting People and Music Through Outreach

L ONG BEFORE THE first notes resounded in the auditorium, a dedicated team was at work promoting Roy Thomson Hall to the city. Volunteer Nancy Westaway was asked by Eugene Blaine, head of project administration, to be a hard-hat tour guide in the summer of 1980. Westaway conducted tours for board members, acousticians, and architects from around the world, as well as for symphony members. When she became overwhelmed with numbers, she remembers "recruiting friends and neighbours to come down to take a peek at our new hall and when they did they were hooked and became the founding force of the volunteers." They also went out to seniors' homes, schools, and services clubs in the search for people willing to help out.

Operating out of a construction trailer at the back of the hall, these music-loving supporters formed the core of what would become the Roy Thomson

Facing page: Children lining up for a concert.

Photo by Richard Beland.

Hundreds of children squeezed onto the stage for a fun and informative workshop with Ivan Fischer, music director of the Budapest Festival Orchestra, 2006.

Photo by Laraine Herzog.

Hall Volunteers, a group whose initiatives laid the groundwork for much of the community outreach the hall engages in to this day.

Douglas Gardner, who has been a member of the Roy Thomson Hall Volunteers for nearly a quarter century, remembers Westaway and the early volunteers as "the hottest, strongest bunch you would ever run into." They were organized and focused, two necessary attributes to help manage the large number of people who were keen to tour downtown's new landmark. Even after it opened, interest in touring Roy Thomson Hall was still high. "We were very busy," Gardner recalls of his early years as a guide. "We had a public tour every day of the week." Some tours reached capacity, and volunteers were often forced to turn people away.

Along with organizing and leading people through the building, volunteers assisted paid staff with a variety of tasks during the 1980s. "Volunteers work for the love of what they do plus the chance to make a difference," noted a column commemorating them at the close of the venue's sixth season. The tasks included staffing the music store and the lobby information desk, and lending a hand with front-of-house duties during concerts.

Volunteers organized and ran a number of special events, and often came up with novel ways to make use of the hall's facilities. These ideas and projects included the Bring Your Own Lunch Concerts held in the north lobby most weeks during the concert season between 1987 and 1996. These concert interludes encouraged

The first of the Bring Your Own Lunch lobby concerts, which featured pianist Francine Kay, 1987.

Photo by Nancy Westaway.

people, as volunteer Doreen Smith wrote, to "drop out of the hustle and bustle" of city life by coming to listen to young artists from a wide range of musical disciplines perform for between forty-five and sixty minutes. Admission was $3 — a pretty good deal for a series that featured performances from an impressive list of young talents that included pianist Stewart Goodyear, soprano Meredith Hall, and baritone Russell Braun.

Another much-loved volunteer initiative was the Salute to Seniors Tea Dance, a regular event that was first held in March 1985. Bus groups of senior citizens would arrive from as far away as Wasaga Beach for an opportunity to snack on sweets made by volunteers, listen to live music, and dance on the stage of Roy Thomson Hall. Many involved, including Doreen Smith, have fond memories of the Tea Dances. "One man on the stage was seen to leave his wheelchair and dance," she wrote. "Two women, meeting casually in the washroom, discovered that they were close friends at school" a half-century earlier. "I think this is one of the best events since the hall opened!" remarked Edward Pickering after attending the second Tea Dance.

Given the success of the Tea Dance, it wasn't surprising that a professionally produced show for seniors came together in 1989. For twenty years, producers Wayne Burnett and Glenda Richards auditioned, cast, coached, and rehearsed seniors from more than seventy-five communities across Ontario, eventually building their "Jubilee" event into a full week of entertainment showcasing singers, ballroom and tap dancers, fiddlers, bands, comedians, and much more. The RBC Seniors' Jubilee not only proved that talent is ageless, but also brought thousands of patrons into Toronto for a week-long extravaganza every August.

Dancers share laughs as they get ready to go onstage at the 18th Annual RBC Seniors' Jubilee in 2006.

Harrison Smith/GetStock.com.

The Roy Thomson Hall Volunteers ushered at many matinees, including the Seniors' Jubilee, assisting the professional front-of-house staff. At their peak, the volunteers numbered more than one hundred and were exceptionally active, often hosting fashion shows or book sales in addition to more regular events. The hall became "our home away from home," Westaway recalls, and "the energy and devotion was breathtaking, exciting and fun."

As membership aged and the hall became a more professionally managed organization, numbers began to dwindle. Although less involved in the day-to-day operations of the hall, volunteers still assist with ushering at matinee performances and during school concerts. They also occasionally still give tours, although hard hats have not been needed for some time.

The volunteers' most enduring contribution to the institution and the greater Toronto music community is the Roy Thomson Hall Award. Begun in 1984, the award was conceived as a way for volunteers to give something tangible and lasting back to the hall by honouring artists, administrators, philanthropists, and

Roy Thomson Hall long-serving volunteer executive members, 2013 (left to right): Janet Watt, Douglas Gardner, and Barbara Bellamy.

Photo by Jag Gundu.

Left: Paula Gomme, president of the volunteer committee (right), with soprano Lois Marshall as she receives the Roy Thomson Hall Award in 1992.

Photo by Brian Pickell.

Right: The Roy Thomson Hall Award is a bas-relief plaque designed by Canadian artist Dora de Pédery-Hunt.

Photo by Matt Barnes.

Judy Simmonds (left) and Nancy Westaway present composer John Weinzweig with the 1991 Roy Thomson Hall Award for his contribution to Canadian music.

Photo by Paul J. Hoeffler.

Lang Lang leads a masterclass as part of his week-long joint Roy Thomson Hall and Toronto Symphony Orchestra residency in September 2008.

Courtesy of the TSO.

volunteers who have made a substantial contribution to Toronto's musical life. As clarinetist James Campbell remarked upon being presented with the 1988 prize, "an award such as this tells you that you are not alone. Someone is noticing your work."

The award itself, a bronze bas-relief designed by Canadian sculptor Dora de Pédery-Hunt, depicts the mythological Greek poet and lute-player Orpheus. It sits in the building's lobby, with each recipient's name inscribed on the base of the sculpture. The list of Roy Thomson Hall Award honourees includes inaugural recipient Victor Feldbrill (1985), Oscar Peterson (1987), John Weinzweig (1991), Maureen Forrester (1998), Molly Johnson (2004), and Jeanne Lamon (2006).

In 2002, administration of the Roy Thomson Hall Award was handed over to the Toronto Arts Council Foundation. Awarded biennially during the Mayor's Arts Awards Lunch, nominations are sought from the public for the award, which now comes with a $10,000 cheque. In 2010, Mayor David Miller spoke at the ceremony about the importance of recognizing members of the arts sector for their work, noting how these individuals "allow us to connect and communicate with one another, and to forge bonds" within and beyond the community.

The connection between the hall and the wider community strengthens each year, thanks in large part to the Share the Music program established by Roy Thomson Hall's director of marketing and development Heather Clark. Designed to inspire and enrich the lives of young people aged eight to eighteen, Share the Music is the cornerstone of Roy Thomson Hall's outreach efforts. Since its inception, the program has provided more than 13,000 concert tickets, free of charge, to schools and community groups.

A Share the Music workshop prior to a concert by Ravi and Anoushka Shankar, 2003.

Photo by Cliff Spicer.

The program had something of a spontaneous beginning. In researching the Boys Choir of Harlem prior to a 1999 concert, Clark learned that its founder, Dr. Walter Turnbull, had established the choir as a means of encouraging young people to stay in school in what was a very tough neighborhood of New York City. "He brought these kids together, taught them how to read music and instilled in them knowledge, pride and self-discipline," said Clark. Following Dr. Turnbull's intervention, the high dropout rate became "an extraordinary annual admittance rate of over 90 per cent going to college. I wanted to share that with students in Toronto." Clark asked local businesses for donations, gave three hundred premium seats for the choir's concert to select schools and community programs, and invited the students and teachers to meet the choristers and Dr. Turnbull following the performance. Despite never having met, many freely shared stories of obstacles they had experienced and overcome. Clark realized that giving Toronto's children and youth a chance to witness a live performance of music they wouldn't normally see or hear shouldn't be an isolated event. The next day she vowed to continue bringing students to concerts at no cost.

Since its inception, Share the Music has expanded exponentially. Now sponsored by Sun Life Financial, it has grown into a program of as many as ten concerts per season across a wide range of events at Roy Thomson Hall, Massey Hall, and the Glenn Gould Studio. Jazz, blues, classical, and world music are all featured, with world music being especially important in a multicultural city like Toronto. Close to two thousand students now participate each year, with 70 percent of available tickets given to schools in the city's priority neighbourhoods, and the other 30 percent

Bobby McFerrin entertains students at a Share the Music workshop, 2012.

Photo by Jag Gundu.

Students at a Share the Music "instrument petting zoo," 2009.

Photo by Lorne Bridgeman.

to arts-focused institutions. Young audience members have responded to the experience enthusiastically. In a glowing testimonial, elementary school teacher Liane Paixão wrote, "For many of our children, just being inside the sophisticated Roy Thomson Hall building was already a special treat, and I'm sure they will cherish those memories." She went on to praise the "many wonderful opportunities to experience beauty through the dance and music performances" her students attended.

Going to concerts is just one part of Share the Music. From the beginning, Clark knew it was important that the program be interactive. As a result, participants attend a thirty-minute pre- concert workshop that gives context to the music they will hear during the concert. Usually, these workshops are led by Toronto-based performers who are experts in the genre of music that is being presented on the main stage. Pre-concert activities sometimes include an "instrument petting zoo," staffed by and compliments of music store Long & McQuade or Musideum, Toronto's rare instrument shop. Brandon, a grade eight student from Ohsweken, a town on the Six Nations Reserve, enthused, "I really enjoyed being able to try out the violins and wind instruments. I never tried any of those instruments until that trip." Grade eleven Lawrence Heights Collegiate Institute student Wes offered what is perhaps an even greater testament to the power of Share the

Music when he said that since attending a performance, he has "given older music a chance," and found that he loves it. Some main stage artists — notable examples are the Canadian Brass, Bobby McFerrin, and Wynton Marsalis with the Jazz at Lincoln Center Orchestra — even give students access to a pre-show sound check or include a private post-concert "meet and greet." All these added components transform the encounter with live music into a deeper and more meaningful experience.

During the 2011–12 season, the program included a non-musical event, and science students were invited to witness former U.S. vice-president Al Gore's multimedia presentation, *Our Choice: A Plan to Solve the Climate Crisis*. Gore also led a question-and-answer period with the students prior to the main event.

Since 2010, Share the Music workshops have expanded beyond the walls of the concert hall — when possible, workshop leaders spend two hours with the students at their schools. "We're hoping to do more of these intensive in-school workshops to support and enhance the work of music teachers in high priority areas," Clark explained. "The in-class format allows young people to engage with the music in a more meaningful way, in small numbers." Margie, a high school student from R.H. King Academy who participated in an in-school string workshop with members of the Toronto Symphony Orchestra, writes that because of Share the Music, she has been "inspired to pursue my love for music and one day perhaps to teach others to love it as well." Music teacher Renata Todros, whose students at Harbord Collegiate Institute have received such in-class workshops as gospel singing and songwriting, is grateful to the program for giving her students "the opportunity of attending incredible performances as well as participating in great workshops. Thanks to Share the Music, my students will have memories for years to come."

The interior space always provides a dramatic backdrop to gatherings and events within the hall.

Photo by Richard Beland.

Laraine Herzog, who joined the Corporation of Massey Hall and Roy Thomson Hall in 1986, has been the coordinator of the Share the Music program since 2001. She believes that the program's success is largely due to the enthusiasm and dedication of music teachers like Renata Todros, who are eager to expose their students to the program's varied offerings. Herzog said that "teachers appreciate receiving invitations for concerts by such diverse artists as classical violinist Itzhak Perlman, flamenco guitarist Paco Peña, and South Africa's Ladysmith Black Mambazo." Herself a musician, Herzog is "delighted to welcome young people to the halls for what can be a life changing experience for them."

The Corporation of Massey Hall and Roy Thomson Hall has focused intently on reaching new audiences since 2008 through the creative use of social media and more interactive presentations. Marketing, publicity, and programming departments have been working together to offer patrons a multi-layered experience that begins before the lights go down and continues long after the last note has been played. Prior to a performance, the public is introduced to artists via podcasts and video featurettes that are posted to *Soundboard,* the corporation's blog.

Although Share the Music and other current outreach programs may seem a far cry from the hard-hat tours and seniors' Tea Dances of the 1980s, they are all born of the same purpose: to encourage the widest possible group of people to know and make use of the hall and its facilities now and in the decades to come.

Luminato 2011 at David Pecaut Square.

Courtesy of Luminato.

CHAPTER 14

A Meaningful and Positive Impact

N O ACCOUNT OF how Roy Thomson Hall came to be Toronto's premier concert venue and meeting place is complete without a tip of the hat to the hundreds of volunteers who worked diligently to turn a dream into reality, and who then had to harness their creativity to ensure that the place would grow and thrive for three decades. These volunteers have served on the board raising funds and ensuring that every community in Toronto is somehow represented in its events and programming. There are also dozens of administrators and other paid staff behind the scenes who have stretched beyond regular work hours and precise job descriptions in order to do their best for the organization and the city surrounding it. Among this army of dedication, certain leaders with particular vision and determination deserve special mention. Foremost among these people is Edward Pickering.

The dapper, businesslike manager died at age ninety-six in his sleep on April 17, 2002, at the Georgian Retirement Home in Dundas, Ontario. It was a deceptively quiet end to a remarkable life that had placed him at the centre of politics, business, and the arts during what Prime Minister Wilfrid Laurier had predicted would be Canada's century.

When he became president of the Massey Hall board of trustees in 1972, Pickering had already spent eleven years on the board of the Toronto Symphony Orchestra, three of those years as president, from 1964 to 1967. During that time, he had made clear his ambition to see a new home built for music in the city. It took fifteen years of non-stop work, all of it as a volunteer, before what became known as

Ed Pickering, chair of the Board of Governors, 1975–88, and president, 1972–88.

Courtesy of Inprint Editorial Services.

Roy Thomson Hall was able to throw open its doors. Pickering led the effort to raise $44 million through the 1970s, a period characterized by the double indemnity of a stagnant economy and high inflation. He navigated treacherous negotiations involving politicians, real-estate holdings, historical boards, architects, engineers, and construction managers, who all brought their own agendas to the corner of King and Simcoe Streets. And, although he was in his mid-seventies by the time the champagne corks popped on September 12, 1982, Pickering would stay on as the head of what was now a two-building operation for six more years.

To describe this man as a doer doesn't even begin to do him justice. "I had seen an awful lot of what happens to people who retire and do nothing," Pickering told writer Adele Freedman in 1983. "They forget they have been working, striving beings all their life, and that can't be turned off. I saw an awful lot of sad things happen to people with nothing to do, nothing to challenge them." And Pickering had always been up for a challenge.

Born in Windsor, Pickering moved to Toronto in 1925 to study political economy at McMaster University (this was four years before the institution moved to Hamilton, leaving its Victorian building on Bloor Street West to become the future home of the Royal Conservatory of Music). He once described the Toronto of the day as "a dull, uninteresting, unattractive, provincial town — and I was coming from Windsor!" So he escaped as soon as he could, landing a job in Ottawa as private secretary to Prime Minister William Lyon Mackenzie King in time for his twenty-second birthday — a job that over the course of the next decade allowed him to meet United States president Franklin Delano Roosevelt, who left him with an open invitation for a personal visit, and, in 1938, German chancellor Adolf Hitler.

Inspired by the federal government's plans to create a national broadcaster, Pickering joined what was then known as the Canadian Broadcasting Commission. In his short time there, he drafted the CBC's rules relating to election broadcasts — guidelines that are still followed today. In 1939, Pickering was taken on by the Robert Simpson Company, a national department store and catalogue retailer that later merged with the Canadian arm of Sears. He retired in 1972 after serving in a succession of senior positions with the company — just in time to dive headfirst into the campaign to build New Massey Hall. In the afterglow of the building's unveiling,

Pickering confessed to Freedman that it had been at once the most difficult and rewarding undertaking of his life: "Many times it looked as though it was going to founder, but our Board of Governors stood firm as a rock. We won over the warm support of hundreds of people and government and private citizens in all walks of life. Working with this 'grand coalition' is the best memory I have of this enterprise."

To professionally manage day-to-day affairs in the building itself, in 1981 Pickering and the board had hired long-time CBC executive Bill Armstrong away from the position of assistant general manager of the English services division. As was the case with so many members of the board that had hired him, Armstrong loved making music as much as listening to it. He was a solid organist, having started with a church job at the age of eleven, and had been involved with many different types of amateur musical and theatrical groups over the years.

Like Pickering, Armstrong was careful to underline that Roy Thomson Hall was not going to be just about classical music, but about programming that reflected all of Toronto. "This is a magnificent hall," Armstrong told CBC Radio broadcaster Clyde Gilmour thirteen months before the new venue opened. "It is not intended to be an elitist structure, exclusively dedicated to so-called serious music. I don't much care for the word 'serious' anyway. Bach was a serious composer, but most of his music can be danced to. Some of the finest works ever written are jubilant and rhythmic." For this general manager, the hall would "cater to all kinds of music that people honestly enjoy. That includes not only symphonic but rock, western and jazz."

Bill Armstrong, general manager of Roy Thomson Hall, with the opening week poster by Nobuo Kubota, which was displayed at transit stops around the city, 1982.

Courtesy of Miles S. Nadel.

Armstrong was lured back to the CBC to become executive vice-president less than a year after opening night and, on his recommendation, was replaced as general manager by Geoffrey Butler, a young, affable arts manager who had successfully opened Kitchener-Waterloo's Centre In The Square. Among Butler's many accomplishments, including working with the Toronto International Film Festival as well as hosting corporate clients, was the establishment of the original international orchestral and vocal series that added so much lustre to Roy Thomson Hall's reputation. Even so, Butler firmly embraced Pickering's and

Geoffrey Butler, general
manager/executive
director of Roy Thomson
Hall from 1983 to 1991.

Photo by Gary Beechey/
BDS Studios.

Armstrong's emphasis of a broad cultural mandate until he was forced to retire
prematurely due to ill health in 1990.

Thanks to Butler's efforts, when Pickering retired as president of the board
in the fall of 1988, he was able to hand over an operating surplus of $771,000 —
generated after retiring a deficit of more than $1 million that Roy Thomson Hall
had run up during its initial seasons — along with a long list of responsibilities,
to successor John Lawson.

Lawson recalls that Pickering

> would arise at 5:30 a.m., cook a steak breakfast, and then write
> out, in his elegant longhand, his reports to the Board, Executive
> Committee, Building Committee, or one of his many speeches,
> ending with tea about 7 a.m. His style was crisp and to the point.
> One day I said to him, "I suppose you learnt to do that when you
> were Mackenzie King's personal assistant." "Not at all," he replied.
> "King's intention was to obscure, mine is to clarify!" An interest-
> ing historical note, which those who listened to King's speeches,
> or read them in Hansard, will appreciate.

Board of Governors, 1987.

Executive team in 1997: Wende Cartwright, Director of Programming; Charles Cutts, President and CEO; Richard Hilz, Controller; Heather Clark, Director of Marketing and Communications; and Susan Jegins, Vice-President, Operations and Administration.

Photo by Gary Beechey / BDS Studios.

Whereas Pickering had a keen analytical mind adaptable to seemingly any subject, including learning the minutiae of how the musical world operates, Lawson came from a background not only steeped in serving Toronto's cultural institutions, but as an active amateur musician who had sung on both the Massey Hall and Roy Thomson Hall stages as a long-time member of the Toronto Mendelssohn Choir, making for a natural connection with the institution and what it represented to the city's cultural life. Lawson's father Hugh had served as chair of the board of trustees of Massey Hall for many years before Lawson was invited to join the group in 1972. The younger Lawson, a partner in the prestigious law firm of McCarthy & McCarthy (now McCarthy Tétrault), had been involved in music since his days at Upper Canada College, performing in the school's annual productions of Gilbert and Sullivan operettas. As with Pickering and all the other members of the corporation's board, Lawson was never paid for his efforts.

As chair of the board's organ committee, Lawson played a key role in pushing for the installation of a symphonic concert instrument in the new building. A few years later, he became intensely involved in the planning and funding of the major festivals organized by Nicholas Goldschmidt. He also helped initiate preliminary studies on improving the acoustics in the venue, began the preparations for the centennial celebrations at Massey Hall in 1994, and spearheaded a major organizational overhaul after Butler's declining health forced him to give up the post of general manager. After taking over the top job in the administration offices at Roy Thomson Hall for four years on a volunteer basis, Lawson oversaw the hiring in

Board of Governors, 1999.

Charles Cutts and
John Lawson.

1992 of Charles Cutts as the first professional president and CEO for the
corporation. Lawson, who took an
early retirement from his law practice,
also made additional contributions
on the boards of the Glenn Gould
Foundation, the Toronto Mendelssohn
Choir, and the Aldeburgh Connection
Concert Society, among others. In
what can only be described as under-
statement, Lawson told an interviewer
in 1993 that he is "totally committed
to the musical life of this city."

Cutts had spent nine years as the
general manager of the O'Keefe Centre
for the Performing Arts (now the Sony
Centre) in the 1980s and two years
with a private hospitality firm when

Richard Balfour, chair of
the Board of Governors,
2010–present.

Photo by Gary Beechey/
BDS Studios.

he took on his new duties at the Corporation of Massey Hall and Roy Thomson
Hall in April of 1992. Lawson remained chairman for several more years. Cutts was
a University of Toronto English literature graduate and Clarkson Gordon–trained
chartered accountant.

"The most significant challenges I've experienced are all people-related," Cutts says, recalling how the first major decision was to reduce overhead by laying off one in four members of the hall's administrative staff due to reporting losses in 1991 and 1992. He also revoked free parking and ticket privileges for all board members. Through the hiring of new programming staff and pushing to have the building's calendar filled on every possible date, Cutts has managed to keep the corporation in the black through his tenure. Cutts says he tries to instill in everyone who works there the sense that they are not working with someone else's money, but their own. That attitude, he adds, is "what gives a hall personality and a soul."

Cutts has been publicly recognized several times for his efforts, most recently in 2012 by the International Society for the Performing Arts and in being awarded Queen Elizabeth II's Diamond Jubilee Medal. As for his own verdict, Cutts lets Roy Thomson Hall's history speak for itself. "Hindsight in our business is the ultimate measure," he says. But a peek into his office overlooking the deceptively peaceful rocks, trees, and water of the North Court reveals clues about the CEO's attachment to the place he has administered for two-thirds of its first thirty years. First to catch the eye are dozens of souvenirs from the entertainment pantheon that has graced the stage a few metres away, including a poster signed by Paul McCartney. Then, placed on the window ledge next to the desk, one can see two big chunks of laminated wood — samples of the materials used in the 2002 acoustical renovation, Cutts's $20-million gamble on the future.

Tim Price, chair of the Board of Governors, 2003–05.

Photo by Cliff Spicer.

Cutts works closely with the members of the board and their committees, some of which include non-board members. With fiduciary and legal trusteeship of the hall at its core, the board has been proud of its wide and interesting balance of professional backgrounds: business leaders, lawyers and accountants, recording industry executives, architects, artists, and community leaders. It's a world away from the early days at Massey Hall, when the first board of trustees consisted of just three people — John Withrow as chairman, Chester Massey as treasurer, and Walter Massey as secretary.

The members of the board of governors in 2013 range in age from mid-thirties to seventies, with diverse backgrounds reflecting the ever-changing Toronto community. Their advisory and stewardship tasks are divided into areas of finance and audit, nominations, programming, development,

As of 2013, staff with twenty-five years of service and more (left to right): Laraine Herzog, Communications Associate and Share the Music Coordinator; Joe Orlando, Usher; Micheal Murphy, Head Stage Electrician, Massey Hall; Nancy Beaton, Venue Manager, Massey Hall; Lillian Thalheimer, Associate Director of Bookings and Event Services; Bruce De La Plante, Building Services.

Photo by Jag Gundu.

Executive team, 2013 (left to right): Heather Clark, Director, Development and Capital Campaigns; Colleen Smith, Director of Operations; Charles Cutts, President and CEO; Liew Wong, Director, Finance and Administration; Jesse Kumagai, Director of Programming.

Photo by Jag Gundu.

arts education, and property. The largest and in many ways most vital committee of the board is the programming planning committee, made up of music industry executives and others who are committed to the musical and cultural life of the city. There are members of the programming planning committee who have served continuously since the opening of the hall in 1982, including Alexander Mair, Suzanne Bradshaw, and John Lawson. The board meets five times a year, while the day-to-day business is left to management. Cutts sums up the expectation: "Here we are, not responsible to shareholders, but to our community. Every day we strive to have a meaningful and positive impact … in a fiscally responsible manner."

The 2002 renovation was the largest board-of-governors undertaking since the building opened in 1982. Despite unanimous board approval of the project in 1998, Cutts would not have peace of mind until he had talked it over with Pickering, who had been privately very disappointed that the building's acoustics hadn't lived up to their original promise. "I had no idea what sort of reaction I would get when I told him that we were going to spend $20 million to renovate the auditorium he had built just twenty years earlier," Cutts told an interviewer at the time. He drove out to Dundas, where Pickering had moved to be close to one of his children. The older man listened attentively, asked questions, and came up with his own assessment. "Charlie, it has to be done," is how Cutts recalls Pickering's response. "Just make sure you do the whole thing. Don't leave it a half measure."

Staff of Massey Hall and Roy Thomson Hall, 2013.

Photo by Jag Gundu.

Roy Thomson Hall
Campaign Committee, 1982

HONORARY CHAIRMEN:
The Right Honourable Pierre E. Trudeau
Prime Minister of Canada

The Honourable William G. Davis
Premier of Ontario

Paul V. Godfrey
Chairman, Metropolitan Toronto

His Worship Arthur Eggleton
Mayor of the City of Toronto

HONORARY TREASURER:
Allen T. Lambert

CAMPAIGN COMMITTEE
CO-CHAIRMEN:
W.D.H. Gardiner
C.E. Medland

VICE-CHAIRMEN:
Edmund C. Bovey
Mrs. M. Suzanne Bradshaw
John E. Brent
Marvin Gelber
Russell E. Harrison
James E. Kelley
Murray B. Koffler
John B. Lawson
Hart V. Massey
Frank F. McEachren
William F. McLean
Trevor Moore
Edward A. Pickering
Mrs. Alexander K. Stuart
Terence A. Wardrop
James W. Westaway
J. Alan Wood

CORPORATIONS CHAIRMAN:
Arthur H. Mingay

FOUNDATIONS CHAIRMAN:
Lawrence Hynes

PERSONAL GIFT CHAIRMAN:
The Honourable Donald S. Macdonald

PUBLIC INFORMATION CHAIRMAN:
Arnold Edinborough

ADMINISTRATIVE CHAIRMAN:
Frank R. Stone

GOVERNMENTS CHAIRMAN:
The Honourable Mitchell Sharp

SEAT ENDOWMENT CHAIRMAN:
Mrs. Judy Simmonds

PUBLIC APPEAL CHAIRMAN:
Murray B. Koffler

EXECUTIVE COMMITTEE:
Marvin Gelber
Chairman

John B. Lawson
Vice-Chairman

Maurice F. Anderson
Edmund C. Bovey
Peter D.R. Brown
Arnold Edinborough
Alexander Mair
Frank F. McEachren
Arthur H. Mingay
Trevor Moore
Mary C. Ortved
Edward A. Pickering
James W. Westaway

BUILDING COMMITTEE:
Edward A. Pickering
Chairman

Walter H. Paterson
Vice-Chairman

Edmund C. Bovey
Arnold Edinborough
Harry H. Edmison
Peter A. Hertzberg
Ross L. Kennedy
John B. Lawson
William F. McLean

OPENING ACTIVITIES COMMITTEE:
Frank F. McEachren
Chairman

Maurice F. Anderson
Mrs. Ann Angell
Mrs. M. Suzanne Bradshaw
Dr. John D. Morrow
Mary C. Ortved
Mrs. Judy Simmonds
Mrs. Alexander K. Stuart
Mrs. John A. Tory

PUBLIC RELATIONS COMMITTEE:
Arnold Edinborough
Chairman

FINANCE COMMITTEE:
Trevor Moore
Chairman

Russell E. Harrison
Vice-Chairman

ART COMMITTEE:
Marvin Gelber
Chairman

SPECIAL EVENTS COMMITTEE:
Murray B. Koffler
Chairman

ORGAN COMMITTEE:
John B. Lawson
Chairman

John Beckwith
George Brough
Andrew Davis
Keith C. MacMillan
Hugh J. McLean
John H. Tuttle

From *BRAVO* magazine,
September 1982,
Issue One, Volume One.

Roy Thomson Hall Enhancement Project Committee, 2002

CAPITAL CAMPAIGN CABINET:

Patsy E. Anderson
Co-chair

John H. Clappison
Co-chair

Ronald W. Osborne
Vice-Chair

Timothy R. Price
Vice-Chair

M. Suzanne Bradshaw
Marcia Lewis Brown
Gordon J. Feeney
Anthony R. Graham
Thomas C. MacMillan
Adam H. Zimmerman

CAPITAL CAMPAIGN VOLUNTEERS:
Geoffrey Beattie
Dean A. Connor
Madeline A. Courey
Robert Cranston
Catherine Deluce
The Honourable Consiglio Di Nino
Stanley H. Hartt
Judith Anne Hinchman
Ross L. Kennedy
John B. Lawson
Yoshio Nakatani
Patricia L. Olasker
Ross Reynolds
John W. Thompson

Charles S. Cutts
President and CEO

Massey Hall
General Managers and Chairmen

GENERAL MANAGERS OF
MASSEY HALL:
Isaac Suckling 1894–1900
Stewart Houston 1900–1909
Norman Withrow 1910–1932
John Carter 1932–1933
Wilfred James 1933–1943
Ross Creelman 1943–1968
Joseph Cartan 1968–1984

After 1984, there was no general manager in the old sense, and management supervision was increasingly exercised by the officers of the Corporation of Massey Hall and Roy Thomson Hall.

CHAIRMEN OF THE BOARD OF
MASSEY HALL:
(in 1982 renamed the Corporation of Massey Hall and Roy Thomson Hall)

John J. Withrow 1894–1899
Walter Massey 1899–1901
Chester Massey 1901–1926
A.E. Ames 1926–1931
J.S. McLean 1931–1954
Frederick R. MacKelcan 1954–1962
Hugh H. Lawson 1962–1973
Edward A. Pickering 1973–1988

Edward Pickering was also president (1972–1988), a new post in which he was succeeded by John Lawson (1988–1992) and Charles Cutts (1992–present).

From *Intimate Grandeur: One Hundred Years at Massey Hall*, by William Kilbourn (Stoddart, 1993).

APPENDIX 4

Trustees of Massey Hall and Roy Thomson Hall Board of Governors

Blaine, Eugene J. 1984–1991

Bovey, Edmund C. 1972–1989

Bradshaw, M. Suzanne 1980–1999

Braithwaite, William 2007– (TSO Liaison)

Brennan, Richard 2005–2007

Brent, John E. 1973–1981

Broadhurst, William H. 1987–1987 (TSO Liaison)

Brown, Peter D.R. 1981–1983

Brown, Marcia Lewis 1994–2004

Burgess, Peter L. 1990–1995

Campbell, Linda C. 1998–

Cartan, Joseph F. 1985–1990

Chant, Diana 2002–2010

Chiu, Yvonne 1997–2009

Clappison, John H. 1991–1999

Coffey, Charles S. 1993–1995

Connor, Dean A. 2002–2005

Cooke, Kim 2012–

Costello, Eileen 2007–

Courey, Madeline A. 1998–2003

Cranston, Robert 1986–1997

Cutts, Charles S. 1992–

Deluce, Catherine 1997–2005

Di Nino, The Honourable Consiglio 1994–2004

Dougherty, Kevin 2012–

Edinborough, Arnold 1973–1992

Edmison, Harry H. 1981–1985

Eggleton, His Worship the Mayor, Arthur 1980–1993

Elliott, Christine J. 2004–2006 (TSO Liaison)

Fatt, William R. 1999–2000

Feeney, Gordon J. 1996–2002

Feldbrill, Victor 1988–1990

Fell, Fraser 2000–2002 (TSO Liaison)

Ferfergrad, Irwin W. 1995–1996

Finkelstein, Bernie 1985–1987

Finlayson, Ian E. 1989–1994

Forrester, Maureen 1980–1984

Forster, David 2010–

Friesen, Eric 2003–2005

Fullerton, R. Donald 1985–1990

Gavelin, Kirby 2003–2012

Gelber, Marvin 1973–1987

Gemmell, Robert 1996–2004

Giles, Jeffrey 1997–1999

Gillespie, Robert T.E. 1991–1993

Godfrey, Paul V. 1984–1991

Goldschmidt, Nicholas 1986–1998

Gomme, Paula 1992–1993

Gopie, Kamala-Jean 2001–2009

Gordon, Lindsay J. 2002–2003

Graham, Anthony R. 1998–2007

Gray, Neil 1999–2000

Haldenby, Douglas C. 1990–1991

Hallman, Eugene 1973–1974

Hamm, Richard 2006–

Hardy, Hagood 1991–1996

Harrison, Russell E. 1975–1984

Hermant, Andrew S. 1986–1998

Hertzberg, Peter H. 1977–1994

Higginbotham, David C. 1981–1994

Hinchman, Judith A. 2001–2003

Horowitz, Aaron 2001–2003

Ignatieff, Helena 1973–1986

Jackman, The Honourable Henry N.R. 1998–2007

Jackson, Fraser 1993–1994

Kearns, Robert 2004–2011
Kelley, James E. 1973–1982
Kennedy, Ross L. 1977–1992, 1995–
    2000 (TSO Liaison)
Kingsmill, A.S. 1990–1995
Koffler, Murray B. 1972–1985

Latimer, Radcliffe R. 1985–1996
Lawson, John B. 1973–1997
Levine, Michael A. 2005–
Louie, Alexina 1992–1999

Macdonald, The Honourable
    Donald S. 1977–1985
MacDonald, Rebecca 2005–2007
Mackenzie, Hugh K.N. 1985–1989
MacKinnon, William 2009–
MacMillan, Thomas C. 2001–2008
MacPherson, Don 1974–1979
Mair, Alexander 1970–1991
Marsden, Lorna 2007–
Massey, Hart V. 1967–1993
Mathur, Chetan 2009–2012
May, Margaret 1994–1995
McCaw, Daniel L. 1997–1999
McEachren, Frank F. 1972–1974,
    1976–1989
McGibbon, The Honourable Pauline
    M. 1972–1990
McKenzie, G.G. 1987–1991
McLean, William F. 1967–1989
Mingay, Arthur H. 1980–1989
Mitchell, Arthur 2003–2012
Moore, Trevor 1973–1984
Morley, H. Keith 1988–1994
Morrow, John D. 1979–1989
Moss, Jacqueline 2009–
Muncaster, J. Dean 1986–1990
Murray, Oliver 2007–

Nakatani, Yoshio 1998–2003
Neish, William J. 1997–2005

Odette, Edmond G. 1985–1990
Olasker, Patricia L. 1998–2006
Olsson, G. Gayle 1999–2003
Ortved, Mary C. 1978–1990
Osborne, Ronald W. 1992–1995,
    1999–2011

Panday, Hari 2004–
Paterson, Walter H. 1973–1984
Pickering, Edward A. 1972–2002
Price, Timothy R. 1996–2007

Reynolds, Ross 2001–2008
Riley, Jean 2002–2003 (TSO Liaison)
Robbin, Catherine 2009–2012
Robertson, Brian 1998–2007
Rose, Barrie D. 1993–1995 (TSO
    Liaison)

Scott, Janet A. 1985–1990
Sherrin, Muriel 1989–1990
Silcox, David P. 1973–1984
Simmonds, Judy 1978–1991
Smith, The Honourable David P.
    2003–2012
Sniderman, Jason E. 1990–1998,
    2001–2008
Sorbara, Joseph 2003–2012
Sorbie, Ian 1995–1996
Stuart, Mary Alice 1974–1988

Taylor, Carole 1973–1976
Thomas, Tom 1992–1992
Thompson, John W. 1993–2002
Thomson, Heather M. 1985–1987
Tory, Elizabeth 1985–1997

Ubukata, Bruce 2001–2008

Vahman, Ash 2012–
Van de Kamer, Ann 1990–1991
Varadi, Ben 2011–

Warrian, Peter 2003–2004
Westaway, James W. 1972–1989
Westaway, Nancy L. 1984–1995
Westcott, James W. 1987–1990
Withrow, John B. 1975–1989
Wong, Dr. Joseph Y.K. 1994–1995
Wood, Donald O. 1990–1991 (TSO
    Liaison), 1992
Wood, John Allen 1972–1981
Wood, Neil 1989–1997

Yamaguchi, Mike 1994–1997

Zimmerman, Adam H. 1992–2002

Roy Thomson Hall Award of Recognition

THE AWARD RECOGNIZES creative, performing, administrative, volunteer, or philanthropic contributions to Toronto's musical life by a person, ensemble, or organization. Established by the volunteer committee of Roy Thomson Hall to thank the community that supported the conception and building of the new concert hall, the award was originally an honorary one. In 2002, the Toronto Arts Council Foundation took over management of the award — it became biannual and a $10,000 cash prize was introduced.

1985   Victor Feldbrill, conductor

1986   Jean Ashworth Bartle, founding conductor of the Toronto Children's Chorus

1987   Oscar Peterson, jazz pianist

1989   James Campbell, clarinetist

1990   William Littler, *Toronto Star* music critic

1991   John Weinzweig, composer

1992   Lois Marshall, soprano

1994   Sponsorship body du Maurier Arts Ltd.

1995   Robert Aitken, flutist, composer, and conductor

1996   The Toronto Mendelssohn Choir and its long-time conductor
         Dr. Elmer Iseler

1997   Joanne Hart and Anne Murdock, founders of Hart/Murdock Artists
         Management

1998   Maureen Forrester, contralto

1999   Louis Applebaum, composer and arts administrator

2002   Roger D. Moore, philanthropist

2004   Molly Johnson, singer-songwriter

2006   Jeanne Lamon, director-violinist, Tafelmusik Baroque Orchestra

2008   Richard Underhill, jazz musician and composer

2010   José Ortega, artistic director of Lula Music and Arts Centre

2012   Lydia Adams, conductor and artistic director of the Elmer Iseler
         Singers and the Amadeus Choir of Greater Toronto

The Corporation of Massey Hall and Roy Thomson Hall Executive Staff

WILLIAM ARMSTRONG, General Manager 1981–1983

JOHN F. BROOK, Director, Special Projects 1987–1991

JAMES BROWN, Director of Finance, Chief Accountant 1991–1993

GEOFFREY F. BUTLER, General Manager/Executive Director 1983–1991

WENDE CARTWRIGHT, Director of Programming, Producer 1995–2000

SANDY CASTONGUAY, Director of Artistic Programming, Artistic Producer 2001–2004

HEATHER CLARK, Director of Marketing and Development 1996–

FRANCINE COLLETTE, Vice President, Sales and Marketing 1993

CHARLES S. CUTTS, President and CEO 1992–

BRUCE DAVIDSEN, Director of Marketing and Special Projects 1984–1986

DAVID DOUCET, Artistic Director, Roy Thomson Hall 1982–1984

ROBERT HALE, Director of Marketing and Communications 1985–1988

SUSAN JEGINS, Vice President Operations, Finance and Administration 1989–2008

JESSE KUMAGAI, Director of Programming 2005–

MARILYN MICHENER, Director of Corporate Development 1991–1992

JANICE PRICE, Director of Marketing Communications 1989–1992

MURIEL SHERRIN, Artistic Director 1990–1992

COLLEEN A. SMITH, Director of Operations 2008–

A. DAVID M. TAYLOR, General Manager 1990–1992

PATRICK TAYLOR, Director of Programming 1991–1993

JOHN WILBUR, Director of Operations 2008

LIEW WONG, Director, Finance and Administration 2008–

INDEX

Page numbers in bold and italics refer to photographs.